SHEBA CHHACHHI

The Tate Photography Series is a celebration of international and British photography in the Tate collection and an introduction to some of the most significant photographers at work today.

Each book focuses on an individual photographer and features a specially selected sequence of photographs, an introduction by a Tate curator, and a conversation with the photographer. These collaborations between living artists and experts enrich our understanding of photography and its connection to everyday life, and move from city streets to seashores, across landscapes and subcultures, through identities and interiors, in a visual travelogue of our world today.

Set against the various social, political and cultural issues of our time, the theme for Series One is Community and Solidarity, which brings together four photographers, unrelated as individual artists yet unified here by their work. A Ghanaian-Russian photographer joins Black Lives Matter street protests in London, an artist-activist in New Delhi chronicles women's emancipatory struggles, a South-African's camera locates queer lives in rural townships, while a Finnish-British photographer captures the community spirit in the North-East of England as perhaps only an émigré can.

Work from several continents is brought together, connected by shared practice. In all of these locations and environments, each imbued with unique struggles and dangers, a commonality of human character and strength inspired by community and solidarity is portrayed, permitting glimpses of joy and hope.

Series One

1:1   **LIZ JOHNSON ARTUR**
1:2   **SIRKKA-LIISA KONTTINEN**
1:3   **SABELO MLANGENI**
1:4   **SHEBA CHHACHHI**

SHEBA CHHACHHI

Edited by
Beatriz Cifuentes Feliciano

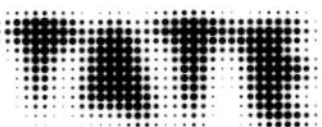

First published 2022 by order of the Tate Trustees
by Tate Publishing, a division of Tate Enterprises Ltd,
Millbank, London SW1P 4RG
www.tate.org.uk/publishing

A catalogue record for this book is available from
the British Library
ISBN 978 1 84976 803 0

Distributed in the United States and Canada by
ABRAMS, New York

Library of Congress Control Number applied for

Series Editors: Simon Armstrong and Yasufumi
Nakamori
Senior Editor: Nicola Bion
Production: Bill Jones
Picture Research: Emma O'Neill
Designed by Sarah Boris
Colour reproduction by Westerham Press, London
Printed and bound in the UK by Westerham Press,
London

Front cover: *Staged Portrait, Nangloi, Delhi* 1980
(see p.25)
Back cover, top: from *The Green of the Valley is Khaki*
1994 (see p.36)
Back cover, bottom: From *Initiation Chronicle* 2001–7
(see p.58)

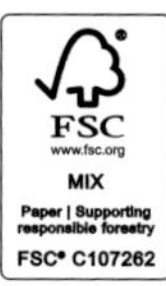

CONTENTS

INTRODUCTION

Sheba Chhachhi is an Indian photographer and installation artist whose works investigate contemporary questions of gender, the body, violence and cultural memory. Born in Harar, Ethiopia in 1958, Chhachhi moved to India when she was three years old. After studying at the Chitrabani Centre for Social Communication in Kolkata and the National Institute of Design in Ahmedabad, she returned to her hometown of Delhi in the early 1980s. Chhachhi began her career as an activist and photographer documenting the Women's Movement in India. By the 1990s, she had moved on to creating collaborative staged photographs, eventually turning to producing intimate sensorial encounters through large multimedia installations.

Chhachhi's works retrieve marginal worlds: of women, mendicants and forgotten forms of labour, and often draw on pre-modern thought and visual histories, interweaving the mythic and the social. First exhibited in 1988, *Seven Lives and a Dream* includes staged and documentary images that span decades of engagement with, and participation in, the feminist movement. Inspired by Subhadra, a woman ascetic, *Initiation Chronicle*, from *Ganga's Daughters*, records the transformation of a group of women sadhus (religious renunciates). Each woman in this series subverts conventional assumptions about gender, sexuality, domesticity and female piety. In the mid-1990s, Chhachhi was one of the first female photographers to photograph women in conflict-ridden Kashmir, resulting in *The Green of the Valley is Khaki*.

SHEBA CHHACHHI
IN CONVERSATION WITH
BEATRIZ CIFUENTES FELICIANO

BCF   Your work gives a voice to the women of South Asia through powerful and intimate photographs and installations. Could you tell us what initially prompted you to document women via photography?

SC   The very first photographs that I made in 1979 were of a woman. I was in training, using a borrowed camera. I used to pass the back verandah of a temple on my way to the Design Institute and noticed this older woman, Subhadra, sitting there, semi-naked. I was fascinated by her elegance, her strong presence. She was a renunciate, an ascetic, and I started dropping in to sit with her. She spoke very little, but accepted my being there. One day I took the camera along and, with her permission, started to photograph. This continued over many meetings.

I have always been drawn to 'odd' women. I feel an affinity, a resonance with women who don't fit the norm – perhaps recognising aspects of myself – and this is reflected in my photographic work.

After the early work that I did with Subhadra, I came back to Delhi in 1980. Here, my sister had co-founded one of the first feminist groups of that time, Stree Sangharsh. I too joined the very powerful, passionate anti-dowry campaign and became part of the resistance to violence against women. I began to photograph our protests, street plays and consciousness-raising workshops ... and found myself doing this for the next ten to fifteen years! I was a participant as much as a documentarian.

BCF   That insider's perspective comes across in the photographs, which convey a strong sense of intimacy. There's an intensity to the images that highlights the depth of your involvement in the Women's Movement.

SC   I would be shouting a slogan one moment and lifting the camera the next! And I was not photographing strangers – these were women that I knew and would meet in multiple contexts.

In the beginning these photographs were for ourselves, a record of the history we were making. Then we began to share these images of the struggle that we were waging against patriarchal, violent regimes with women in other parts of the country, and transnationally as well.

After about ten years of documenting the movement, from 1980 to 1990, I was increasingly troubled by a number of questions about documentary practice and my own work. As a feminist I was analysing power relationships in every sphere – the family, society, the state. However, as a photographer, the power of representation lay firmly with me. While the images I made were an important counter to mainstream representation, I had become painfully aware of the hierarchical relationship that gets set up between subject and photographer. In addition, the nature of documentary practice, where images were presented as objective truth, seemed deeply problematic. It was becoming clearer and clearer to me that there was no medium that was transparent – that everything was in fact interpretative, filtered through subjectivity. It became important to claim that and make it explicit, rather than to further the notion that documentary photography is the truth.

These reflections led me into an experiment. I invited seven women from the movement to work with me, to build collaborative, staged portraits. I was trying to share the power of representation by giving the subject the agency to construct her own image. I also hoped to move beyond the kind of image that I had built up during the previous ten years: that of a militant, protesting, struggling woman. I knew these women as more complex, with histories and narratives which were somehow getting lost or reduced even in my very committed work. It was a rich, intimate process – I spent almost three months with each woman, exploring how we could tell her story, how she wished to appear. It was an invitation to perform the self. We created a series of staged portraits in a variety of locations chosen by the women, and I then placed these alongside photographs of the same women taken over the previous ten years to build a composite portrait of each feminist that brought together multiple images and times. This became *Seven Lives and a Dream*.

BC Could you tell us what solidarity and community mean to you, and how you see these themes reflected in your practice, particularly in *Seven Lives and a Dream*?

SC   Solidarity usually means being one with or in agreement with an event,
            a set of values and so forth. I would expand that notion of solidarity
            to a profound empathy: my photographic work is with women with
            whom I have built intimate, empathetic relationships. I like to think of
            it as an inter-subjective space – a space that we co-create, with both
            subjectivities at play. From that, I let the images arise.

            'Community' is usually tied in with particular identities – religious,
            geographical or historical. But when I look at community in my work,
            I am looking at the sense of community arising from a shared dream
            or vision. If the Women's Movement forms a community, it is through
            the dream of changing women's lives – each individual woman comes
            from a different geography, a different religious identity, a different
            caste or class background, hugely diversified. Yet you are bound
            together by something beyond yourself – by your shared experience
            of patriarchy, by how you understand and critique that, by what you
            dream of as a different possibility. It's that possibility, that vision which
            creates a sense of community.

BCF   Inspired by the renunciate you first encountered as a student,
            you also went on to photograph a community of women ascetics.
            Could you describe the process these women undertake?

SC   Ascetics step out of conventional definitions of gender identity.
            They leave their families – they are no longer mothers, wives, daughters
            – and that alters their entire location within the social fabric. Their
            initiation process is an extraordinary stripping away of all the markers of
            gender. The initiate gives up her clothes, her hair, her name, her family
            name and the community she belongs to. She performs death rites for
            that social self and makes offerings to seven generations of ancestors
            before she is reborn as a renunciate. This process takes place along
            the river, immersed in water, and she is reborn as a daughter of the river.
            Often, the new name the woman renunciate receives is the name of a
            river – which is why my series is called *Ganga's Daughters*.

            The process of initiation is private and secret, and I was honoured
            to be allowed to witness it. Several groups conduct initiations
            simultaneously along the bank of the river, and I was with one
            particular group whose initiates were all comfortable with me
            being there. Women guards patrol the area to ensure that nobody
            – especially men – comes close. I had to be very discreet, and was
            semi hidden under a pile of blankets. At one point, one of the blankets
            slipped as I was photographing, and I suddenly felt a hard blow on my

back. A woman guard had hit me! I put the blanket over my head again and disappeared while the leader of my group mollified her. A narrow escape from being beaten by the guard's stick!

The *Initiation Chronicle* follows this moving, very special, powerful process. The reborn, re-named woman takes on the robes of, and is presented to others of the particular sect she has been initiated into. Often she takes on an androgynous appearance.

BCF   So this is their new community.

SC   The kind of community that gets constructed is very interesting. The women who have taken this path have done so through choice or circumstance – they could be escaping violent situations, abandoned, or simply women who do not wish to marry. Alongside these are women who feel a genuine spiritual call. There are fewer women ascetics than men, but they're still a very substantial number. They form a sorority within the larger spiritual community. During the huge gatherings of the whole spiritual community they have their own enclave and their own place in the ritual processions.

However, it is not a settled community for the most part. One of the freedoms that these women acquire is mobility. They travel alone, in pairs and in groups, something that ordinary middle-class and working-class women can't do with ease in this country. But the renunciates are women on the move, visiting ashrams and pilgrimage places, and travelling around the whole of India. When the weather gets bad, they go to a place connected to their sect where they will always get shelter until they head off again.

During my research I found this ancient text – a sort of code of conduct for Hindu housewives. It says: 'If a male sadhu comes to her door, a good housewife must welcome him as an honoured guest, feed him and serve him.' However, if a female sadhu comes, she should close the door and not have any conversation with her.

BCF   Oh!

SC   She's dangerous, you see. A good housewife might get ideas.

BCF   I think this goes back to when you referred to these women ascetics as early feminists, since even historically they were women that had agency. They sat outside the conventional society and its gender-based expectations and rules. Most of the accounts we have are from a male perspective and reference men's accomplishments, so it is always so interesting when one can gain insight into the lives that women were living – not just those who lived life as was expected of them, but also the ones that managed to live 'alternative' lives …

SC   And radical lives! These are radical lives and radical statements. Some of the early poetry of women ascetics is extraordinary. These Vachanas – small poetic, philosophical texts composed and sung by wandering women saints – are from around the twelfth to sixteenth centuries, but they're very contemporary in their sentiments. There's an even earlier one, from the sixth century, which says:

> So free am I, so gloriously free
> Free from three petty things –
> From mortar, from pestle and from my twisted lord
> Freed from rebirth and death am I
> And all that has held me down
> Is hurled away.[1]

The women that I photographed are not saints, but it is the poetry, and the stories of their lives that inspired me.

BCF   And the poetry is in part how you got into the project?

SC   In the early 1990s, I came upon the powerful poetry of rebel, mystic and poet Akka Mahadevi. I was struck by the bringing together of the erotic and the spiritual, the scathing rejection of conventional female roles, the articulation of the body-self relationship – her voice was absolutely contemporary!

I quote:

> Not one not two
> not three or four,
> but through eighty-four hundred thousand yonis [vulvas]
> have I come,
> guzzled on pleasure and on pain.

And there were others. Compelled by these glimpses of indigenous, premodern forms of feminism, I began researching women ascetics from ancient and medieval India. There was very little sociological work at the time, but I found a rich repository of poetry, stories, images and hagiographies from the sixth century onwards. Some of these texts were retrieved by feminist scholars ; others I found through oral traditions, visual representations and popular songs.

BCF   You did all this historical research, which speaks to your in-depth and intimate approach when photographing.

SC   I read everything I could find! This process, like in a lot of my work, stretched over ten years. Meanwhile I would meet and spend time with the women renunciates, then, maybe a year later, when they were gathering again, I would reconnect with them.

BCF   Now if I may shift focus, perhaps we could talk a little bit about the Kashmir series.

SC   When we come to the Kashmir situation, 'community' becomes even trickier to define. These are women in a conflict situation and the conflict has drawn hard lines between communities. In the mid 1990s, the news and the images we were getting of Kashmir were dominated by men with guns – the army, the border security forces, the militants waging war for independence. Women, if mentioned at all, were described as victims or fundamentalists. Four of us – we called ourselves the Women's Initiative of Kashmir – decided to go into the valley to try to speak with women and find out how they saw the conflict. We were entering a tense, possibly dangerous situation. Obviously, I could not build the long relationships I often do in my work. We had to work hard to gain trust. We weren't just outsiders, we were from India, which at the time was represented by this brutal occupying force in Kashmir. As we travelled around the valley meeting and speaking with women, we offered our solidarity as women, irrespective of religion or nationality. I photographed during these intense, emotional exchanges, always with their consent and sometimes active participation.

BCF   You were in fact one of the first female Indian photographers in the area. Perhaps the fact that you were a woman enabled you to gain the trust of the Kashmiri women in the midst of all the terror and the difficulties their community was facing?

SC   Yes. Today there are several young Kashmiri women photographers telling their own story – but at the time most photographs of Kashmir were taken by male journalists, both local and international.

However, when I describe the women in the photographs as
a community, that is entirely my perception. They don't see
themselves as a community. I see them as a possible community
forged through traumatic experience – an experience shared on
both sides of the division that has been created between Hindus
and Muslims. I have seen instances of this in other conflict zones –
in Sri Lanka, for example, Tamil and Sinhala women came together
because they had shared experiences and problems. The conflict
was experienced by them as women, not only as Tamil or Sinhala.
The same happened in Rwanda. In all these places, this meeting
across the divisions of man- made wars has been fueled by a desire
for peace and the knowledge that military solutions are not going
to lead anywhere.

This was something that all the Kashmiri women that I spoke to
also felt strongly, whether they were Hindu refugees in a camp,
Muslim women who had gone through terrible experiences at the
hands of the army, Sikh women who had been dispossessed,
Muslim women whose brothers, husbands, sons had become
militants... It was a very wide range of identities, including women
who were different types of Muslims, even though we tend to see
Muslims as homogenous. Kashmiri tradition has a long syncretic
history, with a strong Sufi and mystic influence. Across all these
different communities, the women were connected to each other
by their compassion and dignity in the midst of conflict and their
rejection of violence as a solution.

BCF   This series on Kashmir was actually an installation.

SC   The installation *When the gun is raised, dialogue stops ...,*
        a collaborative work with Sonia Jabbar, invites the viewer to enter
        the private spaces of war, to 'hear' the voices of the ordinary women
        of Kashmir, normally drowned out by the clamour of stereotypes.
        We were interested in creating a 'third' space outside the polarities
        which characterise representations of the Kashmir conflict.

        We worked with humble materials – earth, bricks and rice to
        evoke the domestic – and used a configuration that draws on
        the contemplative formalism of the Mughal gardens in Kashmir.
        'Books' of rusted iron are placed within a series of book holders,
        each displaying a black and white photograph and a testimony.
        These testimonies were gathered over a decade. The structure of
        the installation itself brought about a realisation of the commonality

in what all the women were saying, despite their differences, reflecting my perception of them as a 'community' seeking peace.

The first version was shown in the Peace Tent at the 1995 International Women's Conference in Beijing, where I met women from Rwanda, Ireland, and other conflict regions. After Beijing, we set up another version in the corridors of the Hague Appeal for Peace in 1998. The installation had a strong activist history before it came into art spaces in 2000.

BCF   The project also evolved with time.

SC   Yes, over time it became more streamlined and, I think, a stronger installation. The last iteration continues to travel. In fact, it was shown quite recently, at the Chennai Photo Biennale in 2019, and still, unfortunately, had great relevance.

BCF   Especially in light of what has happened politically in Kashmir and Ladakh over the last few years. But this work, though it has travelled, has not been widely published.

SC   That is correct. One of my concerns throughout my practice has been the way people look at photographs. We are continuously inundated with photographs, and in a gallery most people spend only a few seconds looking at an image before moving to the next. One of the reasons I began creating photo-based installations was to try and change that quality of attention – to slow people down, to offer photographic images in a way that produced more sustained engagement beyond simply getting information: instead, I want the experience to be about accessing the deeper layers of meaning within the image, to reinvest the viewing of photographs with time.

This was especially important when it came to sharing images from a conflict zone. We had text and image, exactly like the mass media, so for us it became very important to create a different viewing relationship , to make possible an intimate encounter with each image, each testimony. The 'books' enabled this.

BCF   This feature reminded me of book holders for the Qur'an.

SC   Indeed, these are used for the Qur'an and the holy books of every religion. It is somewhat subversive to insert rusted iron sheets into these! Because of the low platform, you must bend down to see these – the body is brought into the act of looking, and this helps concentrate the attention. The reception of image and text is different from encountering it on a wall. I think this, along with other elements of the configuration, worked well: the quiet concentration was palpable when I watched people within the installation. I was therefore reluctant to publish the images in any other form. Some excerpts have featured in a feminist diary, and one or two other publications. But it has not been published as a body of work before now.

BCF   I think in terms of audiences, publishing the photographs will increase their reach. How exciting that we are witnessing a new chapter in the life of this very powerful series.

Just as a closing question, I wanted to ask about your future work and what you're currently focusing on. Can you tell us what direction you're moving in?

SC   I have been engaged with questions of ecology for the last decade or so, and that concern only becomes more urgent. I have also been experimenting with devices which animate still images, kinetic sculptures and video. I moved to installation in the early 1990s, because of wanting to change the relationship with the photographic image. Then I began working with digital images, where I fused historical iconography with photography. My practice today is cross-disciplinary, in every respect – medium, vocabulary, ideas. I photograph less, in the sense of creating bodies of photographic work such as those we have talked about. However, the photographic image – found, made, historical or contemporary – still lies at the heart of what I do. For the moment it is a more frugal relationship to photography, perhaps because we are surrounded by an excess of it.

1   'Mutta', from Therigatha: Songs of the Nuns, circa sixth century BCE.

SEVEN LIVES AND A DREAM

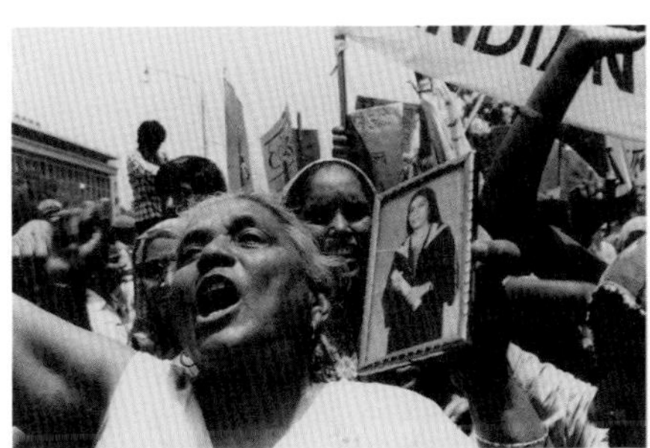

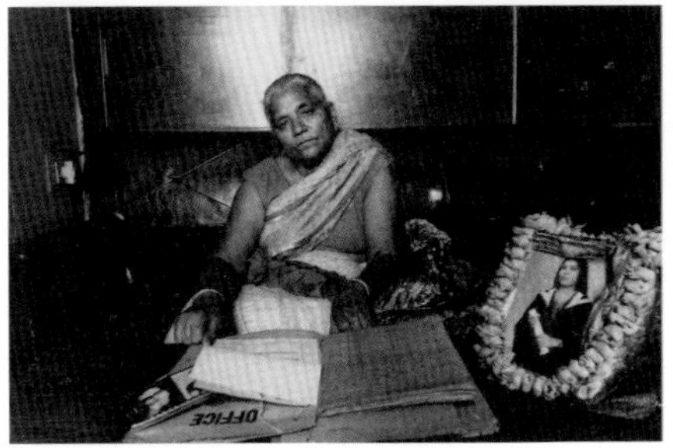

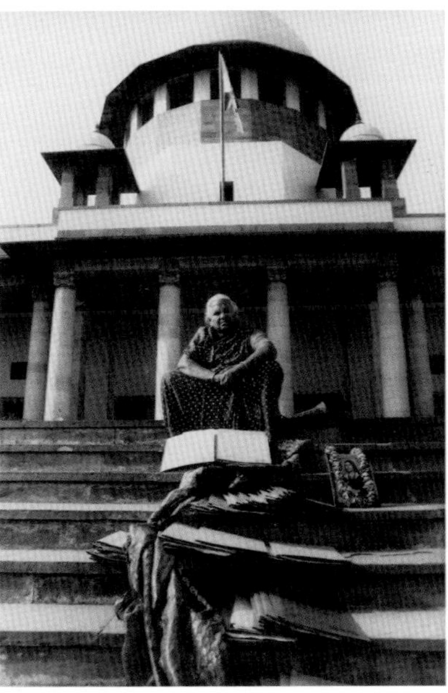

Sathyarani
Anti-Dowry Demonstration, Delhi 1980
Staged Portrait, Supreme Court, Delhi 1990
Staged Portrait,Punjabi Bagh residence 1990

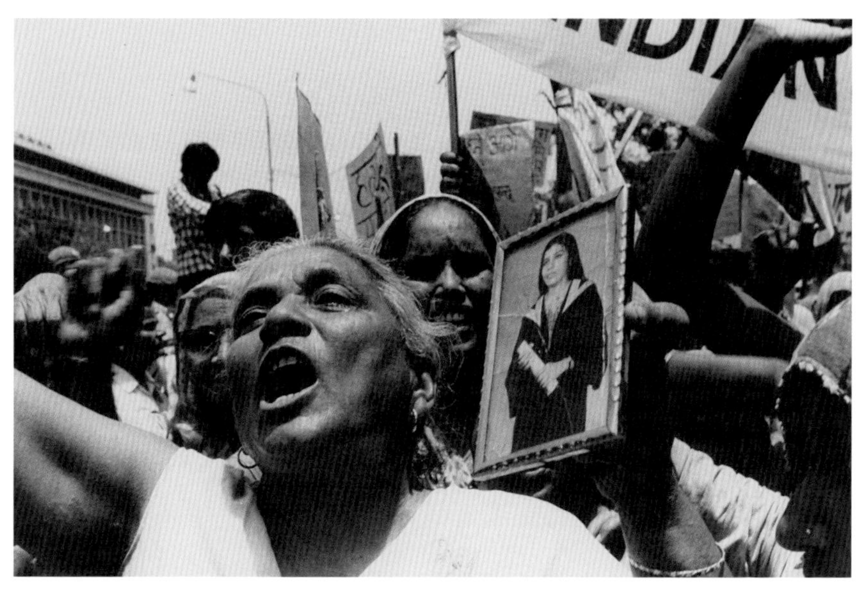

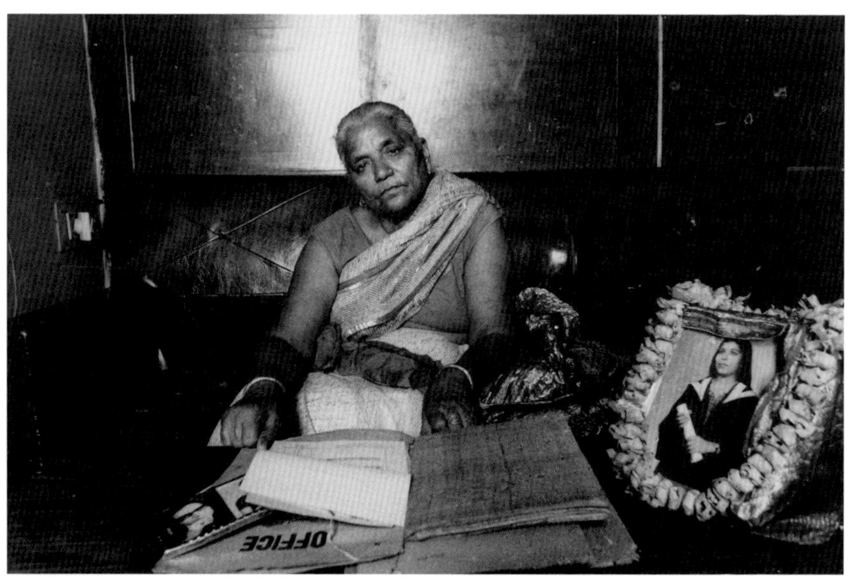

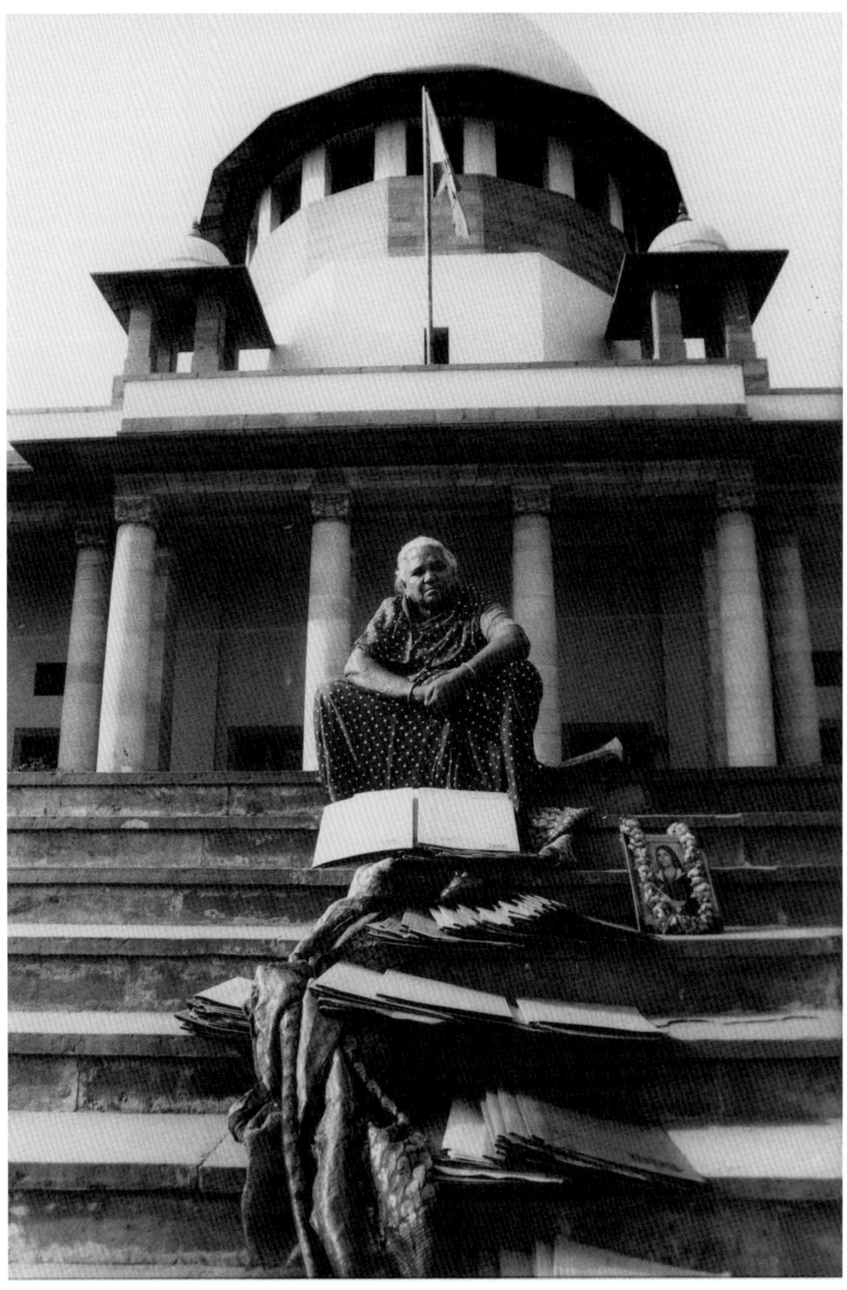

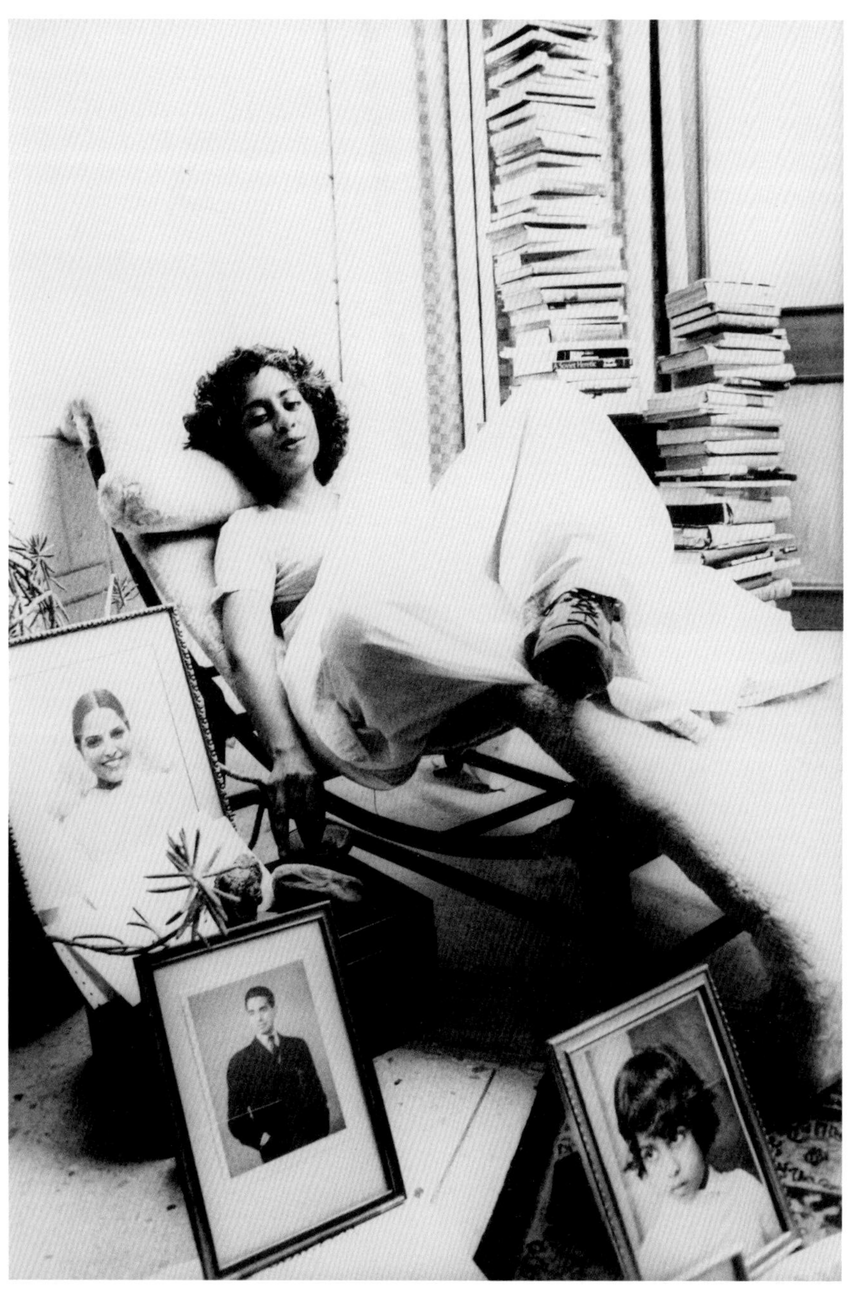

Radha
Staged Portrait, Anandlok 1991
Staged portrait set up, Anandlok 1991

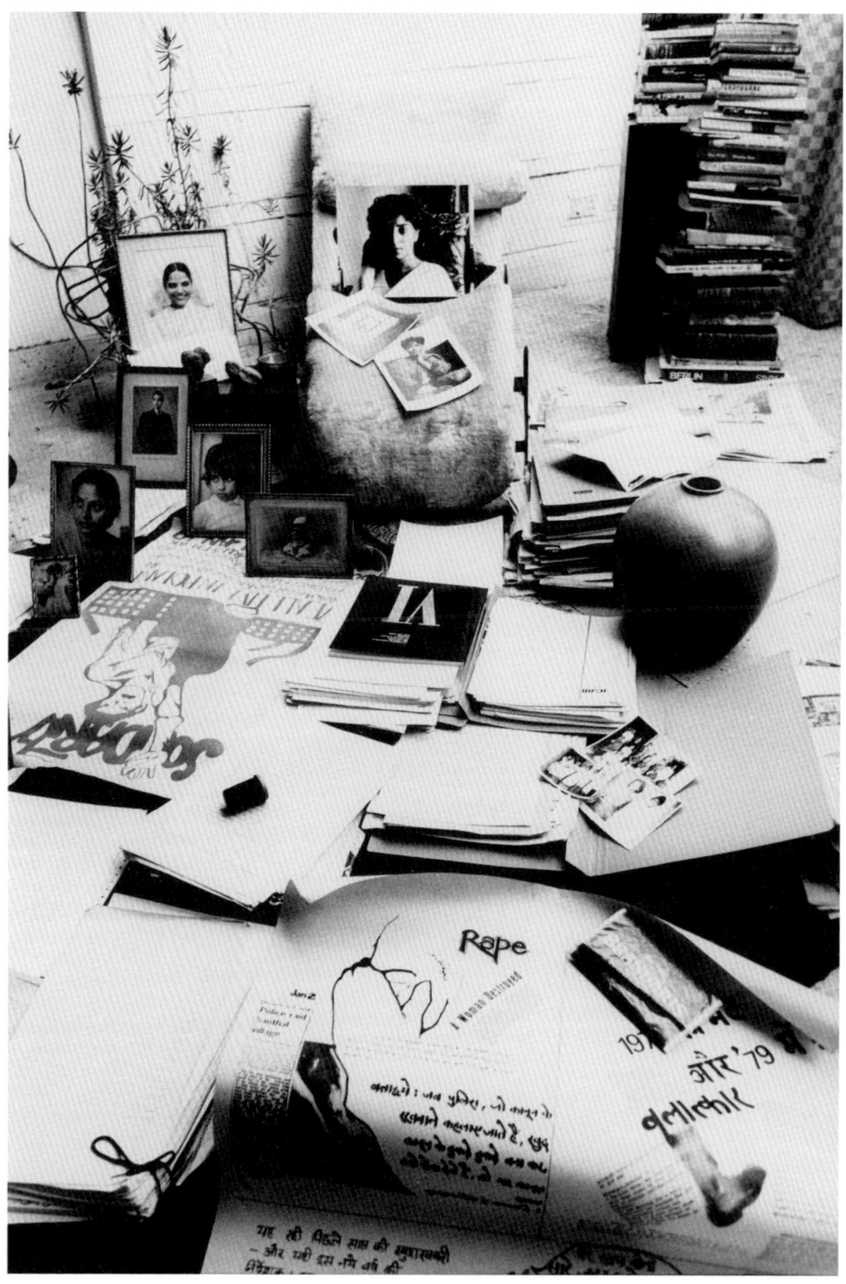

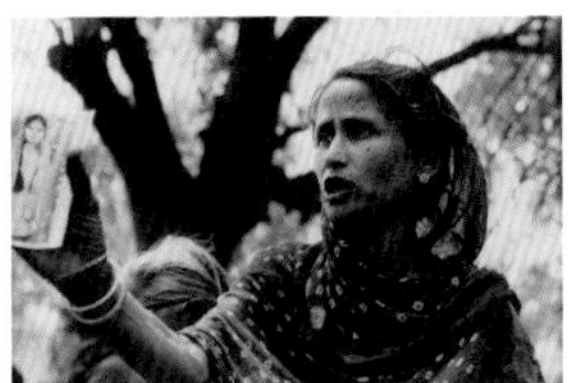
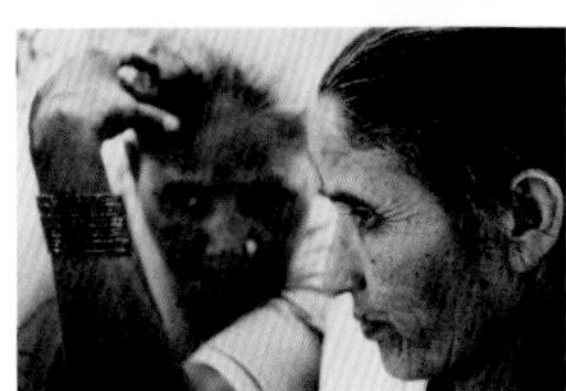
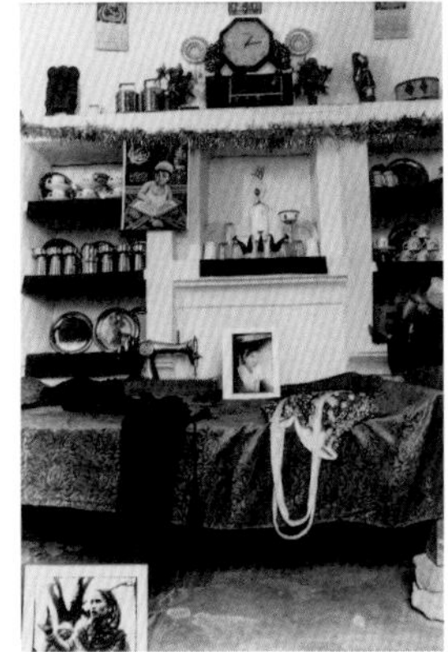
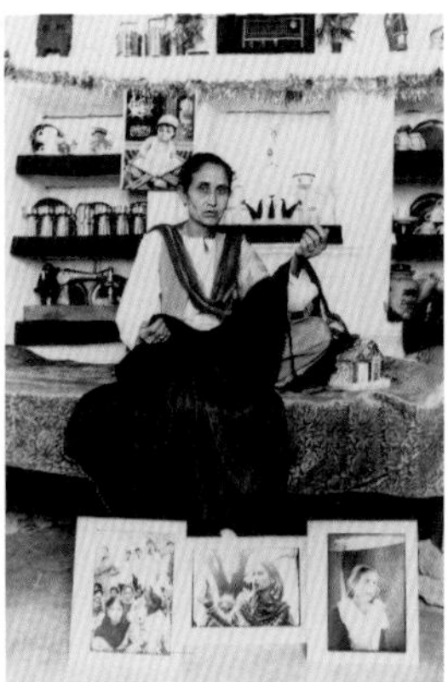

Shahjahan Apa
Anti Dowry Public Testimonies, India Gate, Delhi 1980
International Women's Day gathering, Dakshinpuri, Delhi 1986
Staged Portrait set-up, Nangloi, Delhi 1991
Staged Portrait, Nangloi, Delhi 1991

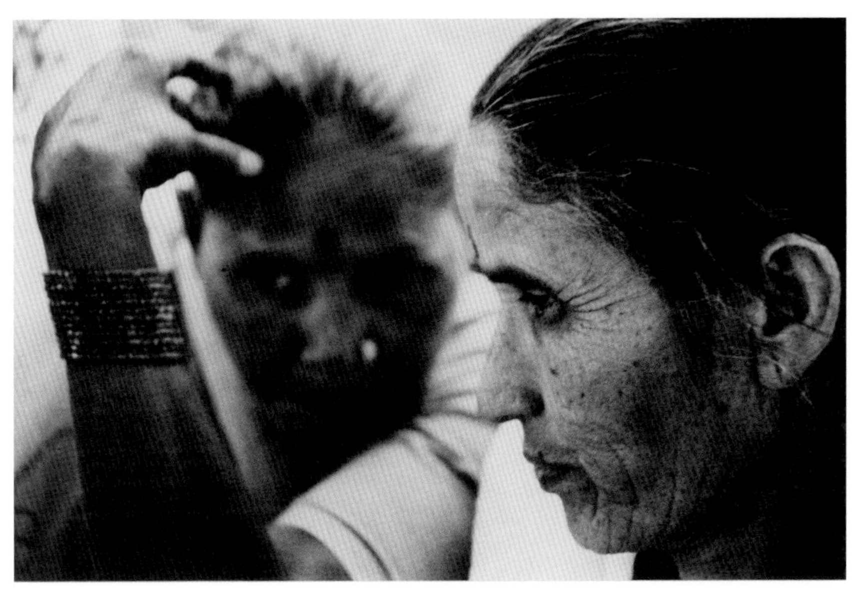

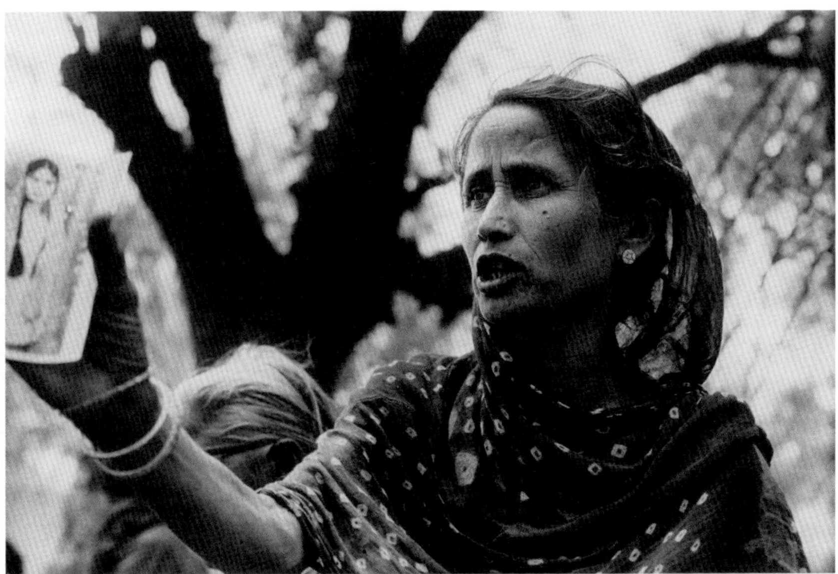

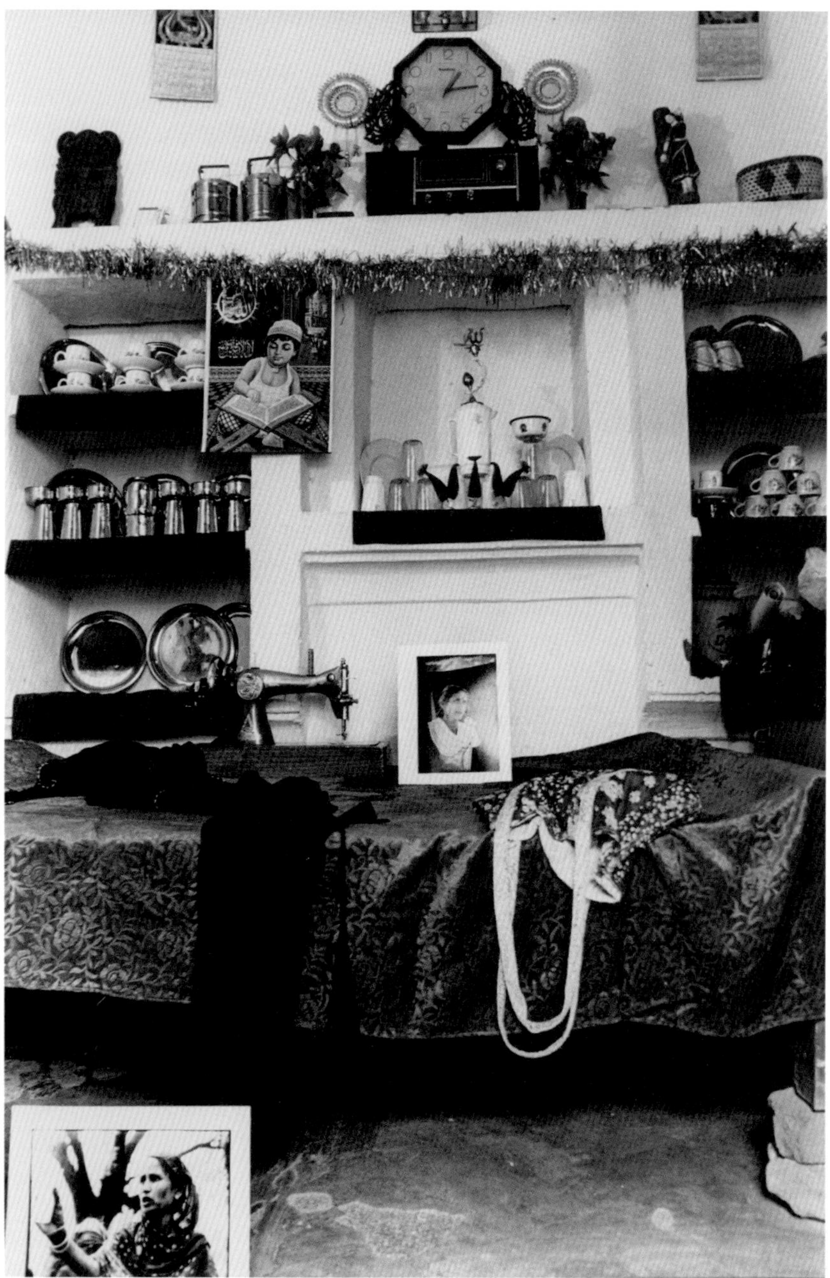

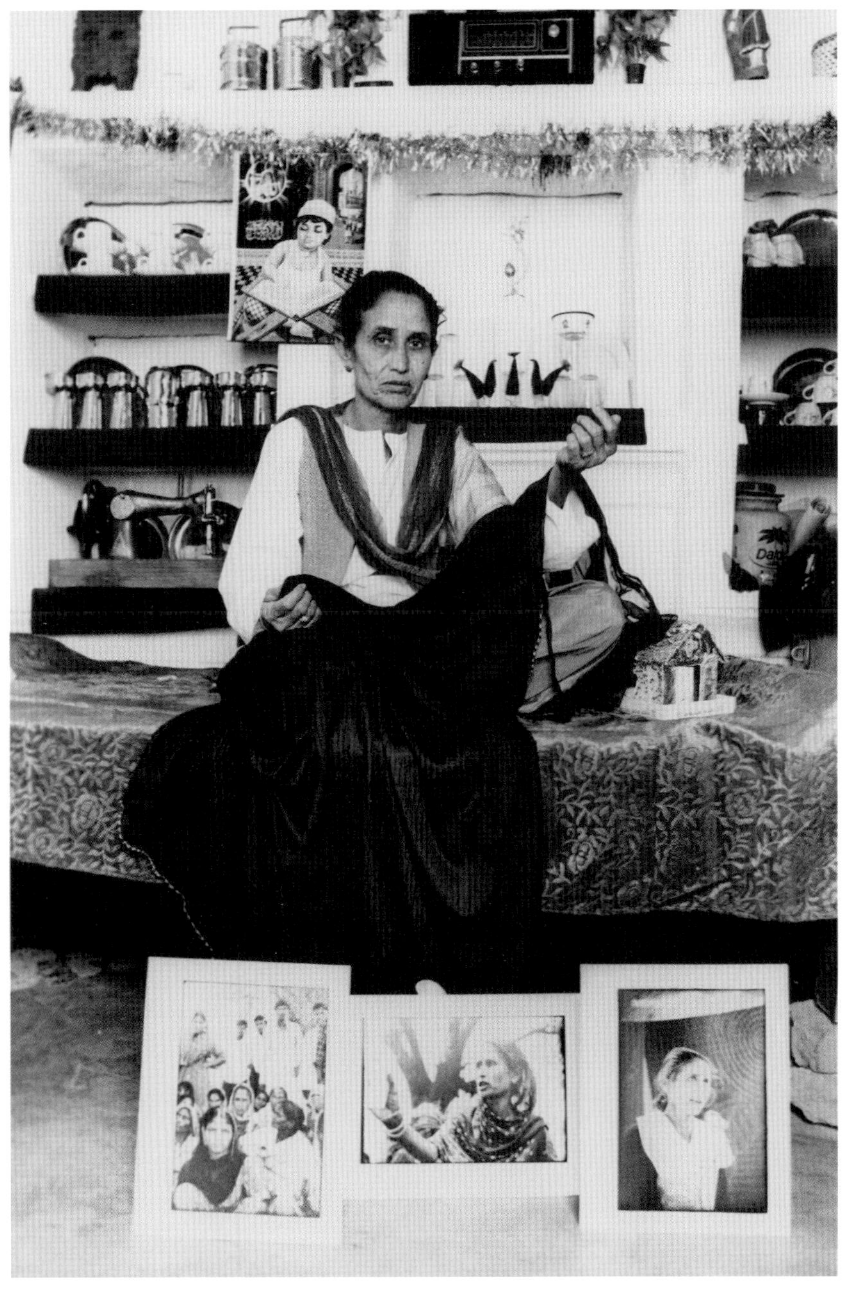

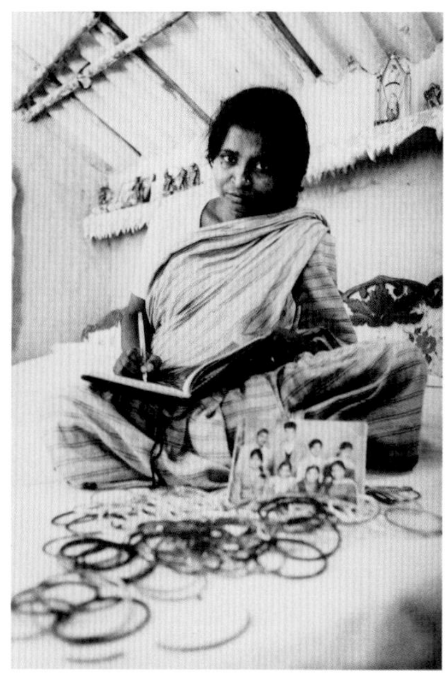

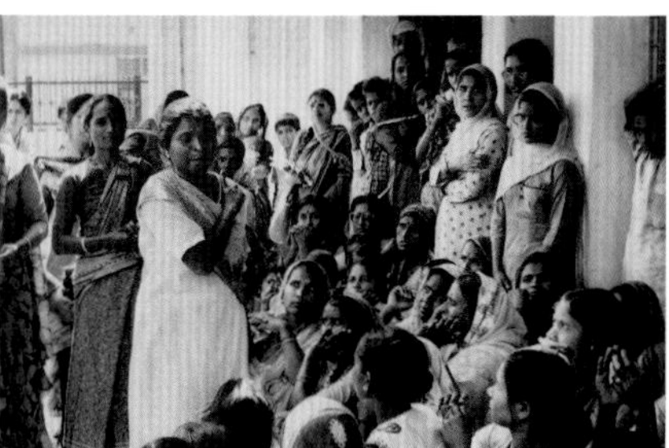

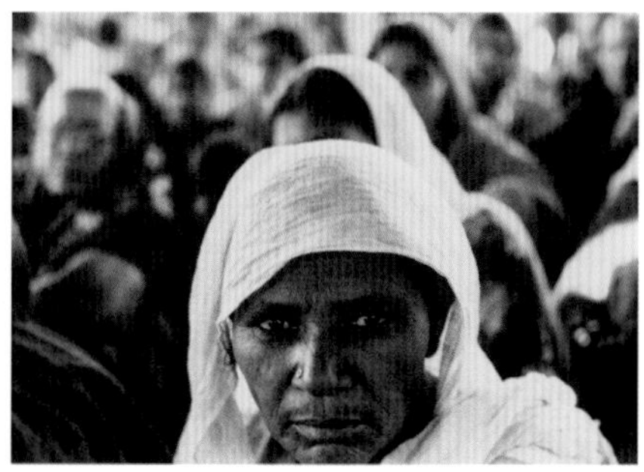

Devikripa
Staged Portrait, Seemapuri, Delhi 1990
Sitin, Family Planning Centre, Nandnagari, Delhi 1988
Women's movement meeting after Sikh pogrom, Delhi 1985

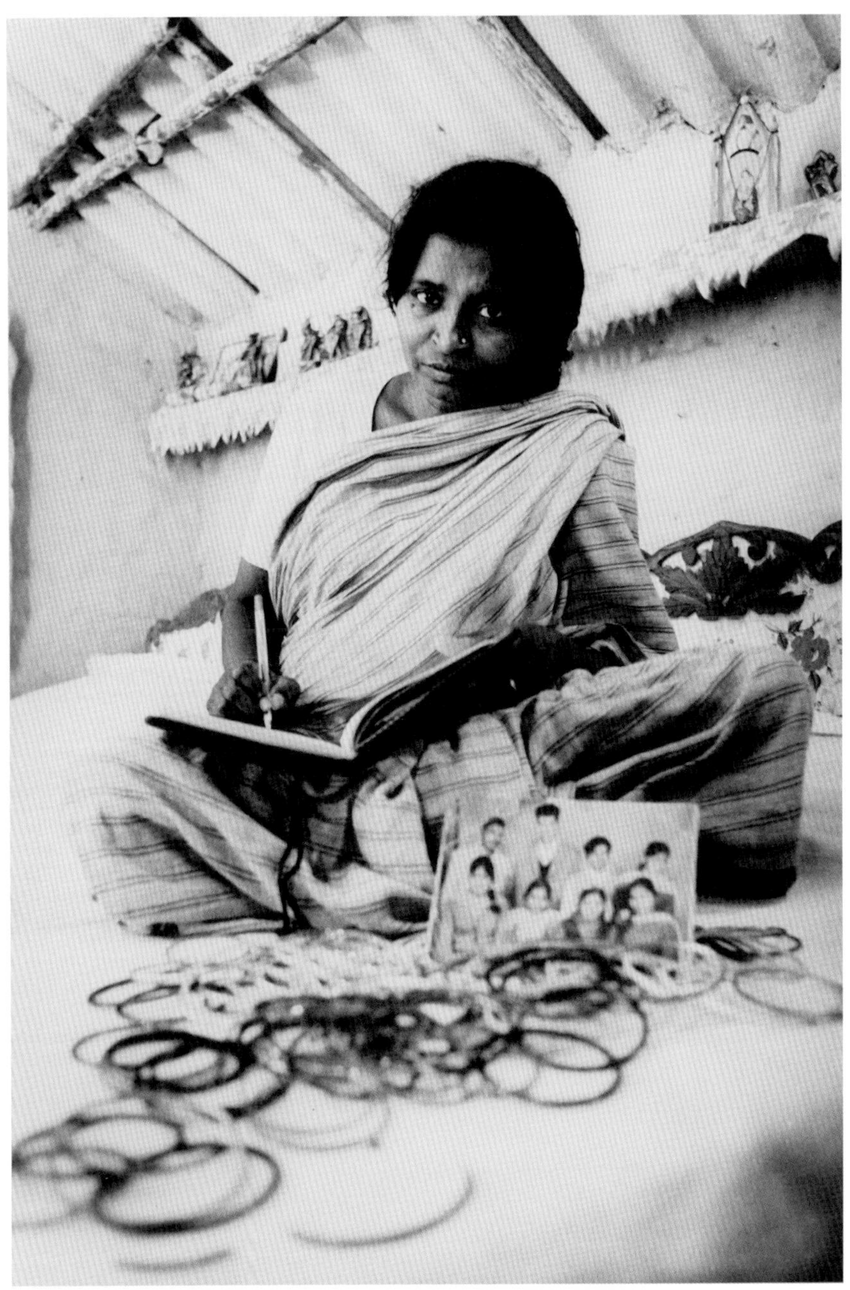

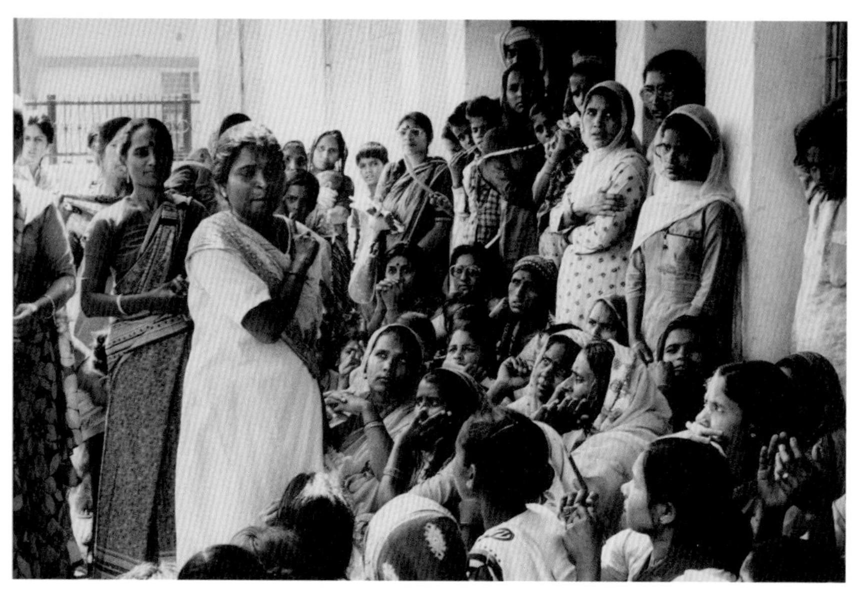

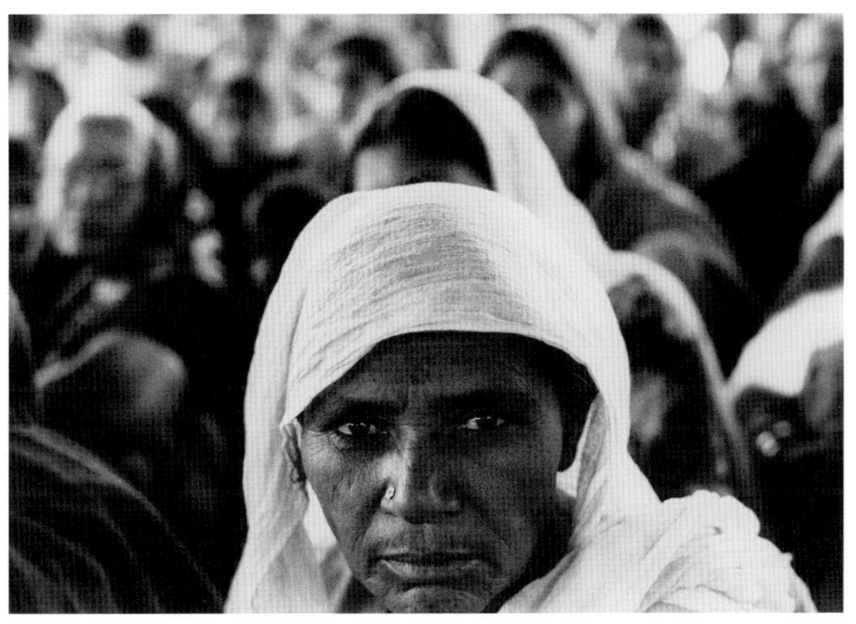

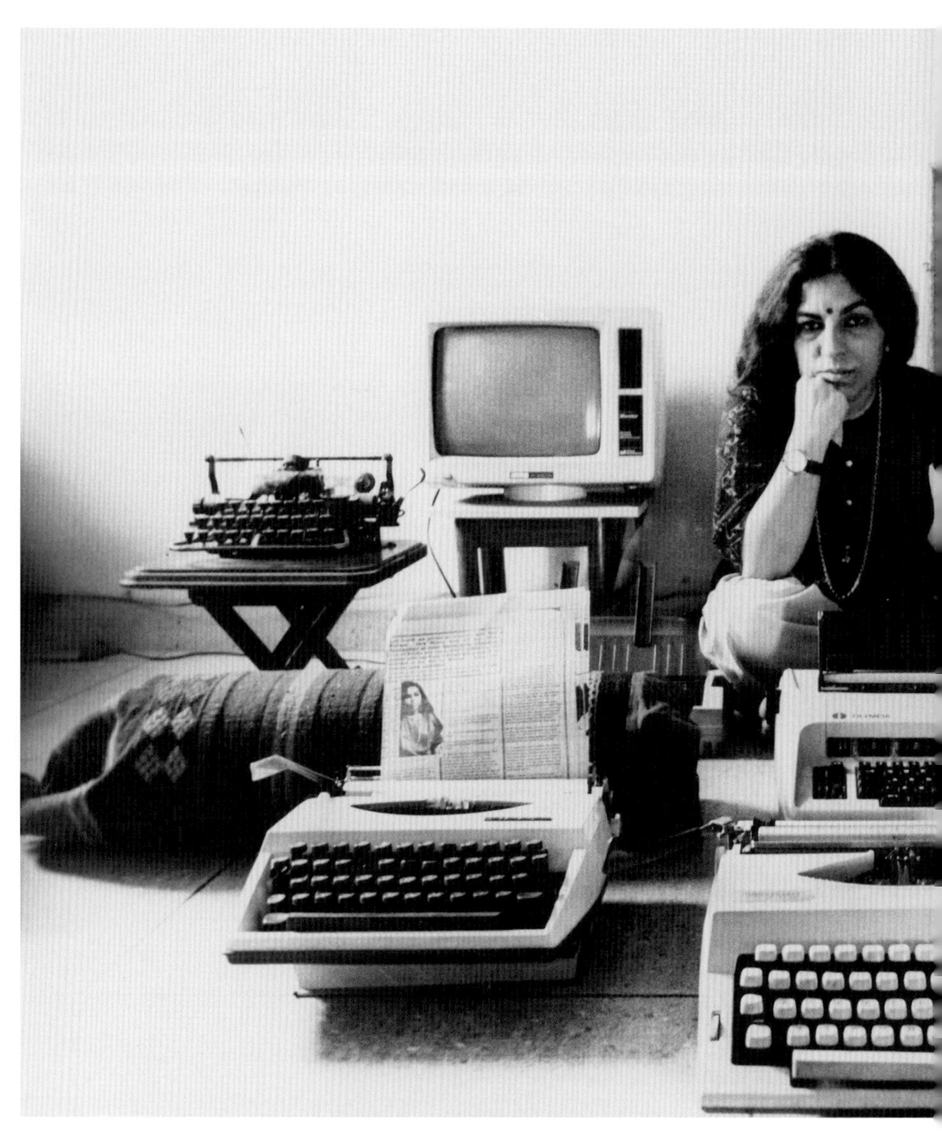

Urvashi
Staged Portrait, Gulmohar Park, Delhi 1990
Sit-in outside Police Station, Nangloi 1981
Anti-Dowry street play 'Om Swaha', India Gate 1982

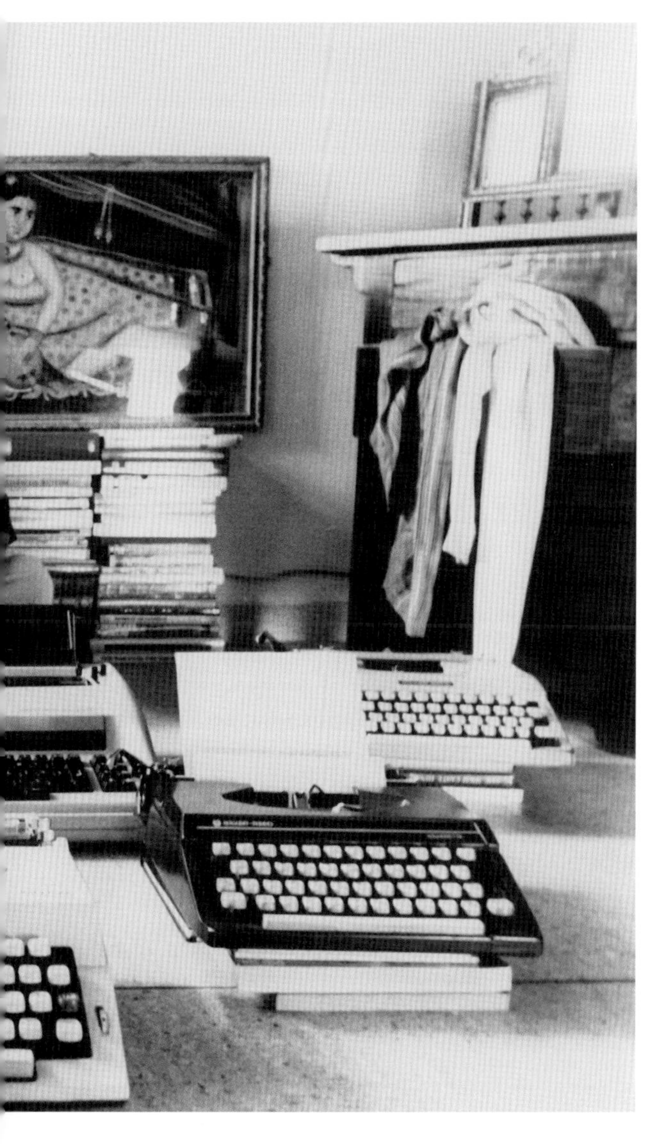

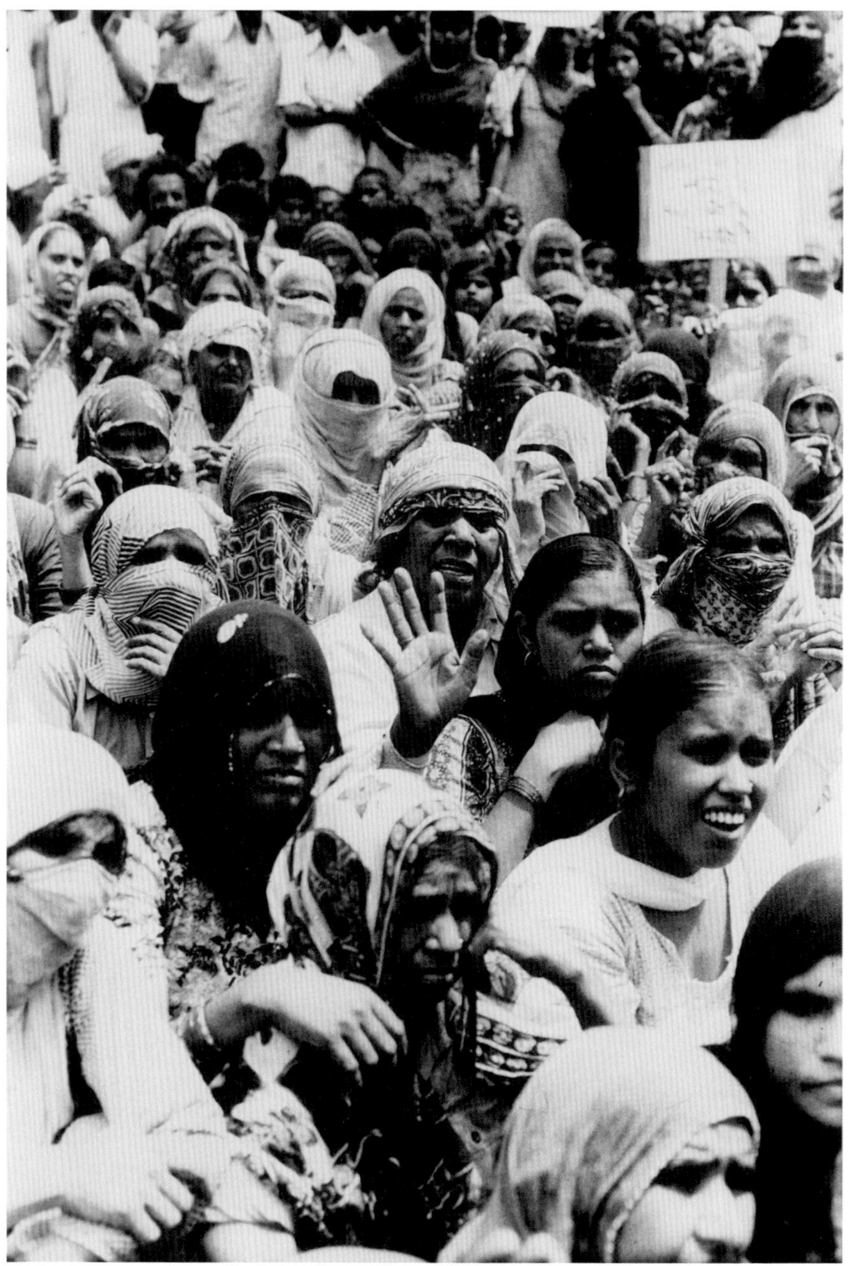

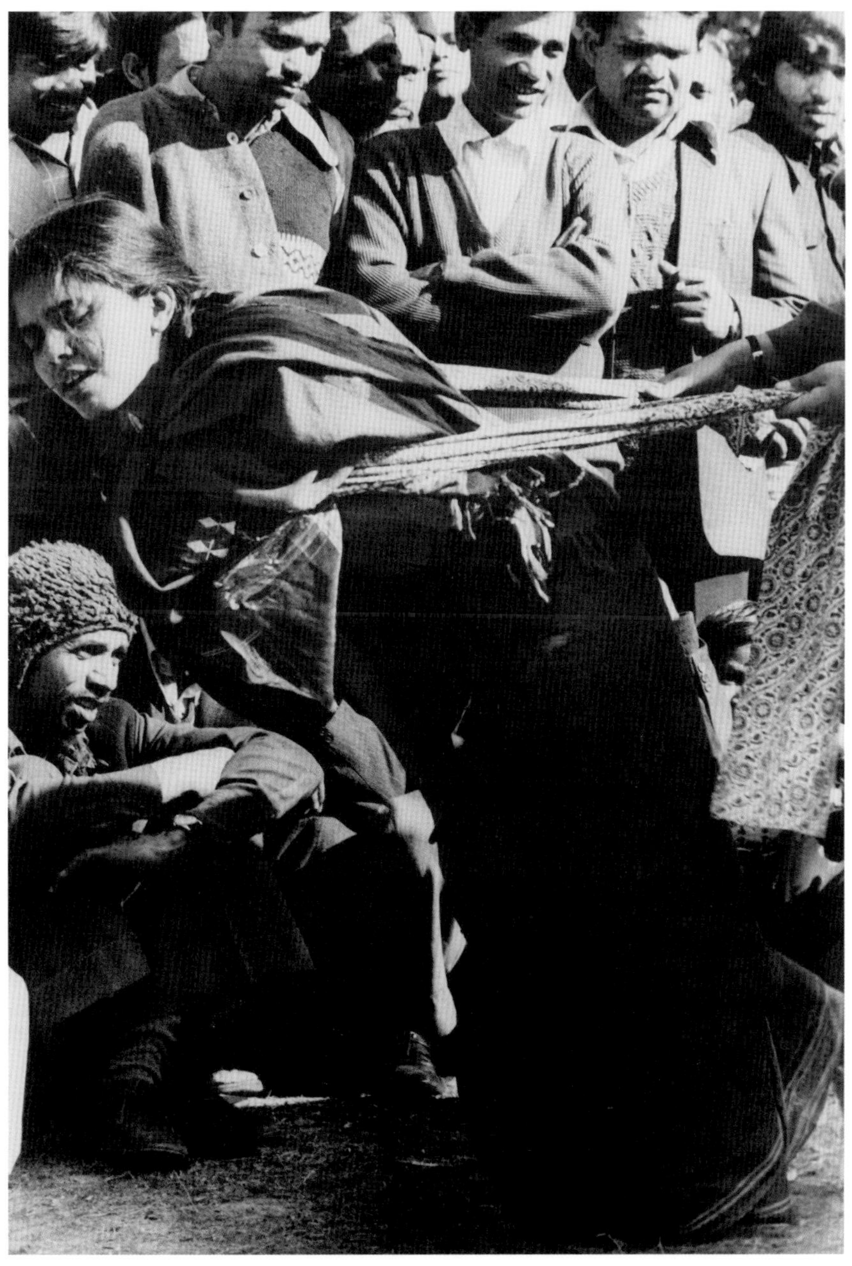

THE GREEN OF THE VALLEY IS KHAKI

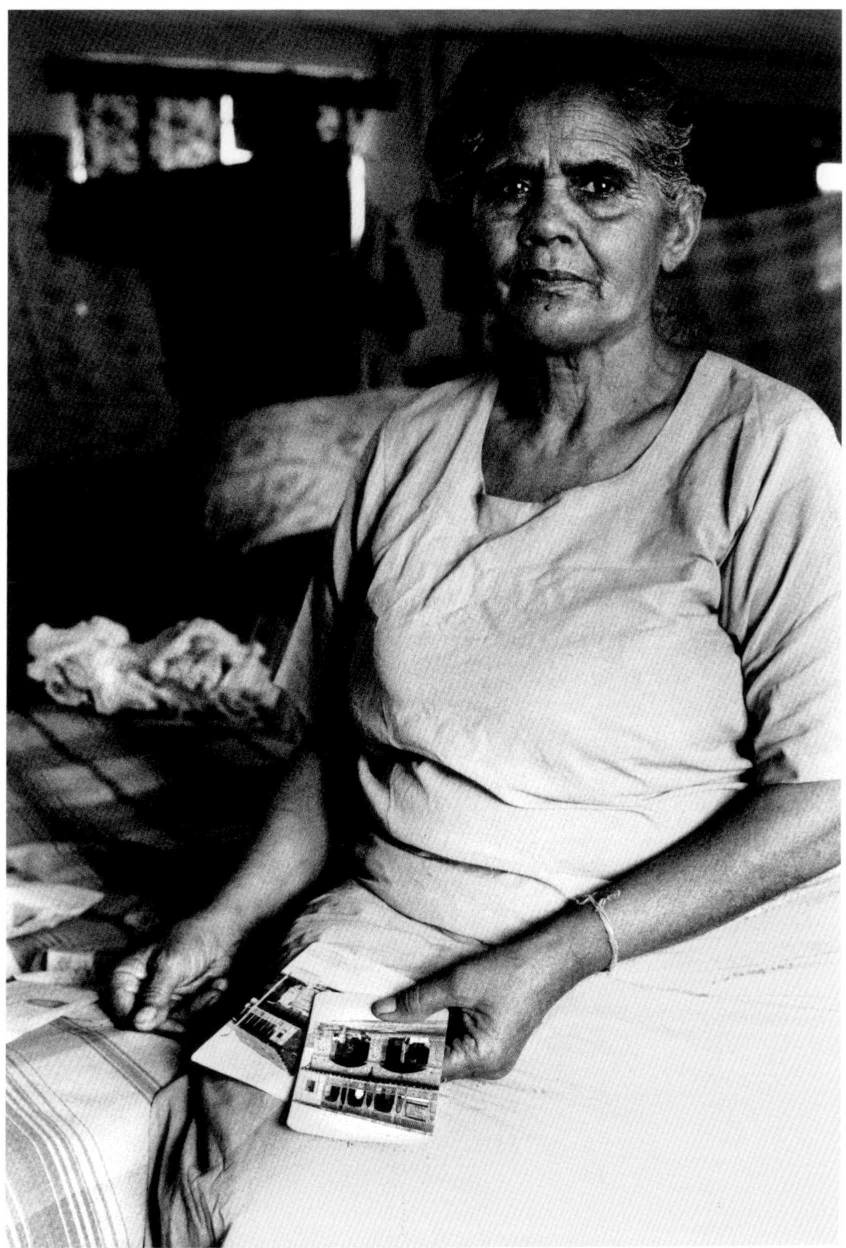

  Ajit Kaur, Jammu Refugee Camp

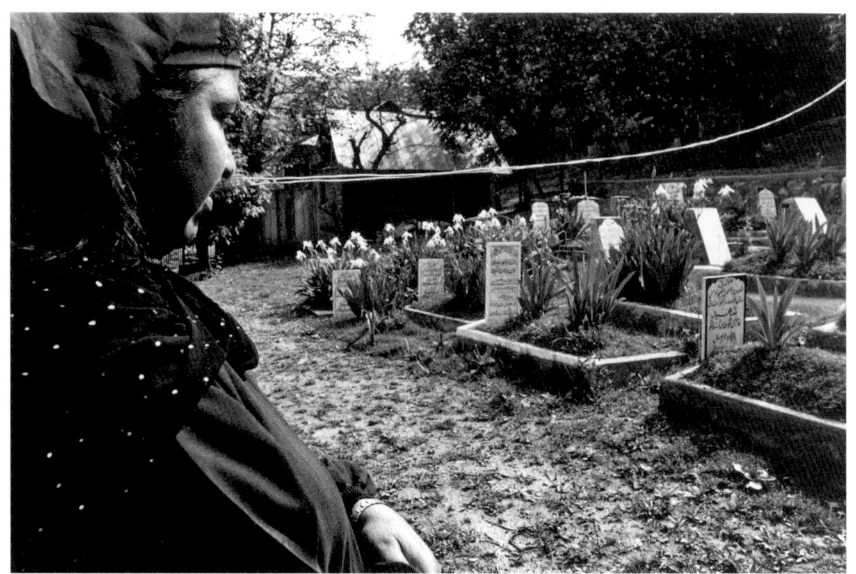

     Saira at the Martyr's graveyard, Bandipora, Kashmir

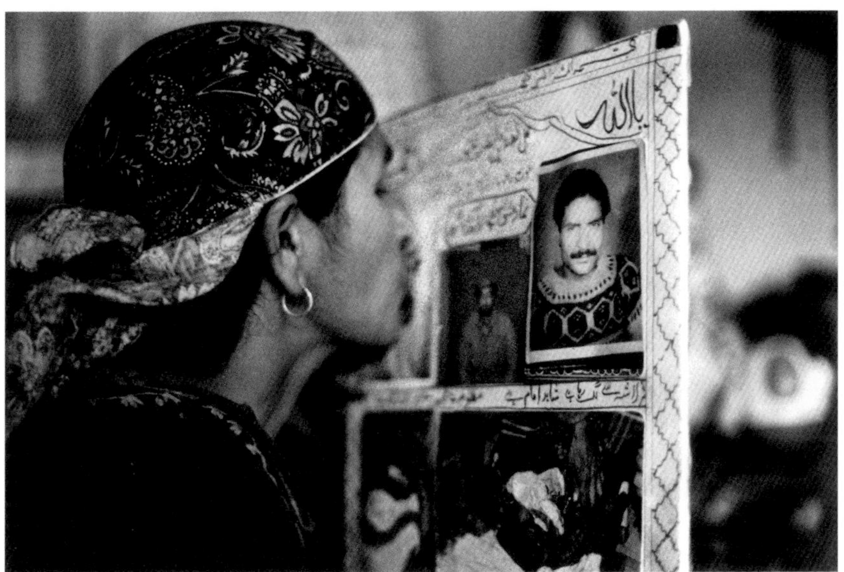

 Jameela, widow with collage of her husband's photos, Malangam, Bandipora, Kashmir

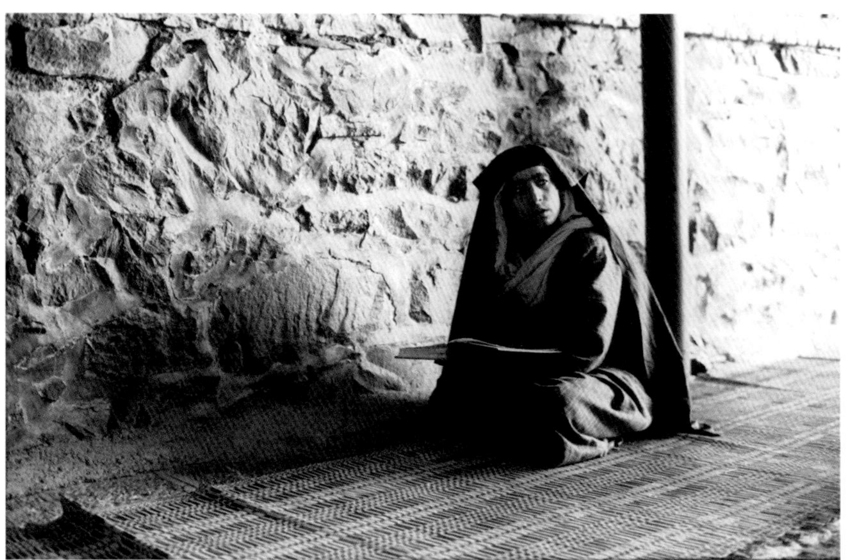

   Mediator at Makhdoom Sahib, Sufi shrine, Srinagar, Kashmir

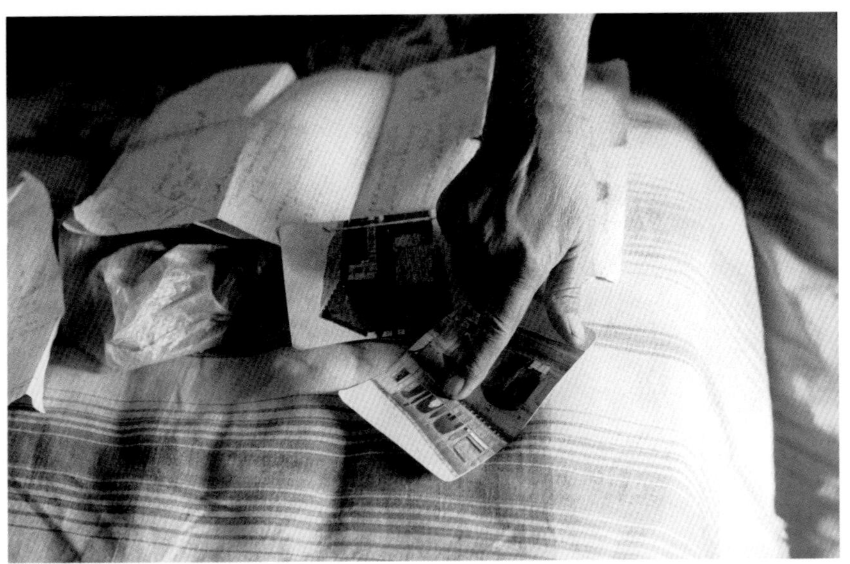

   Abandoned Pandit home, Jammu Refugee Camp, Jammu

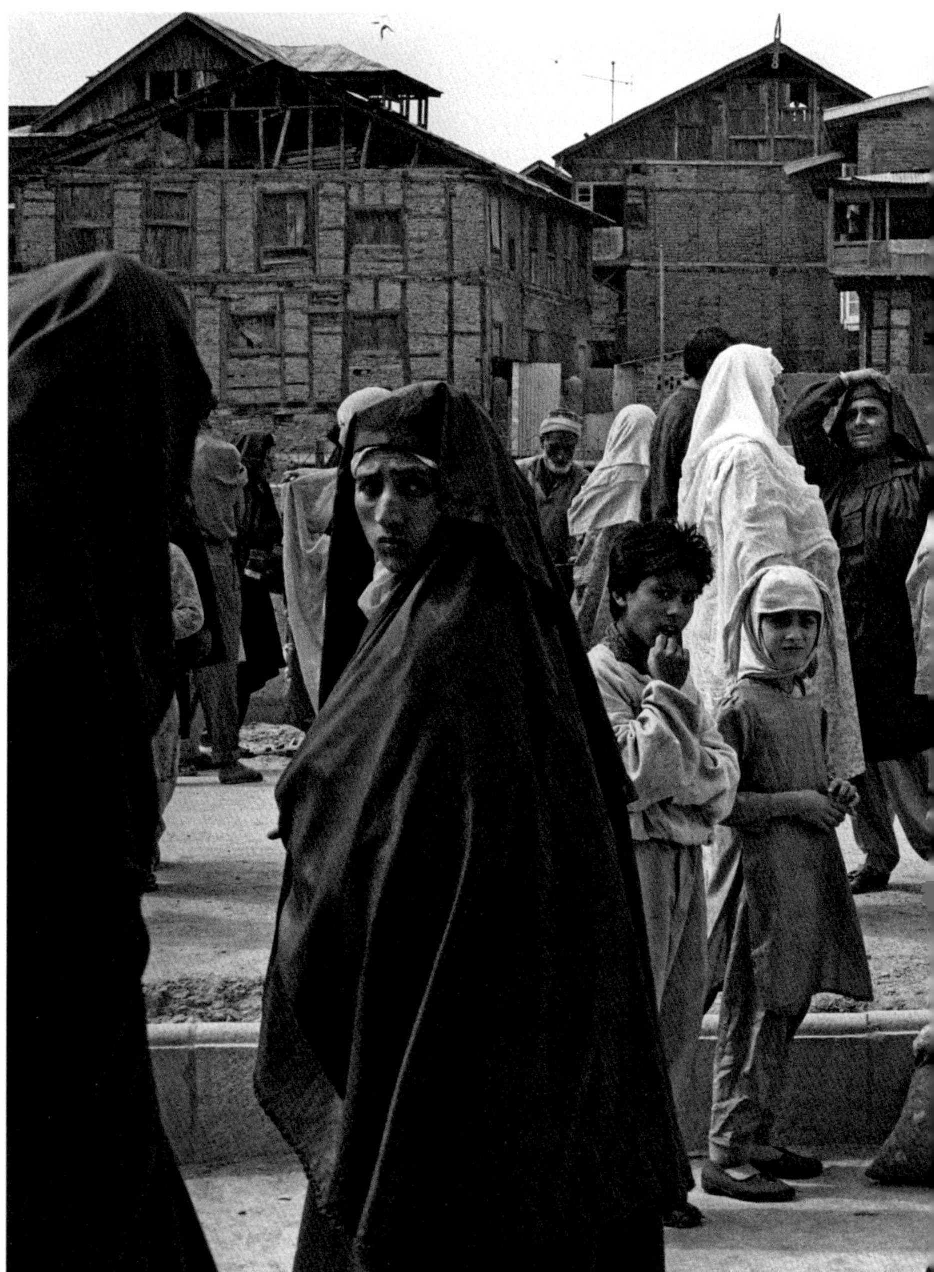

  Outside 14th-century mosque, central Srinagar, Kashmir

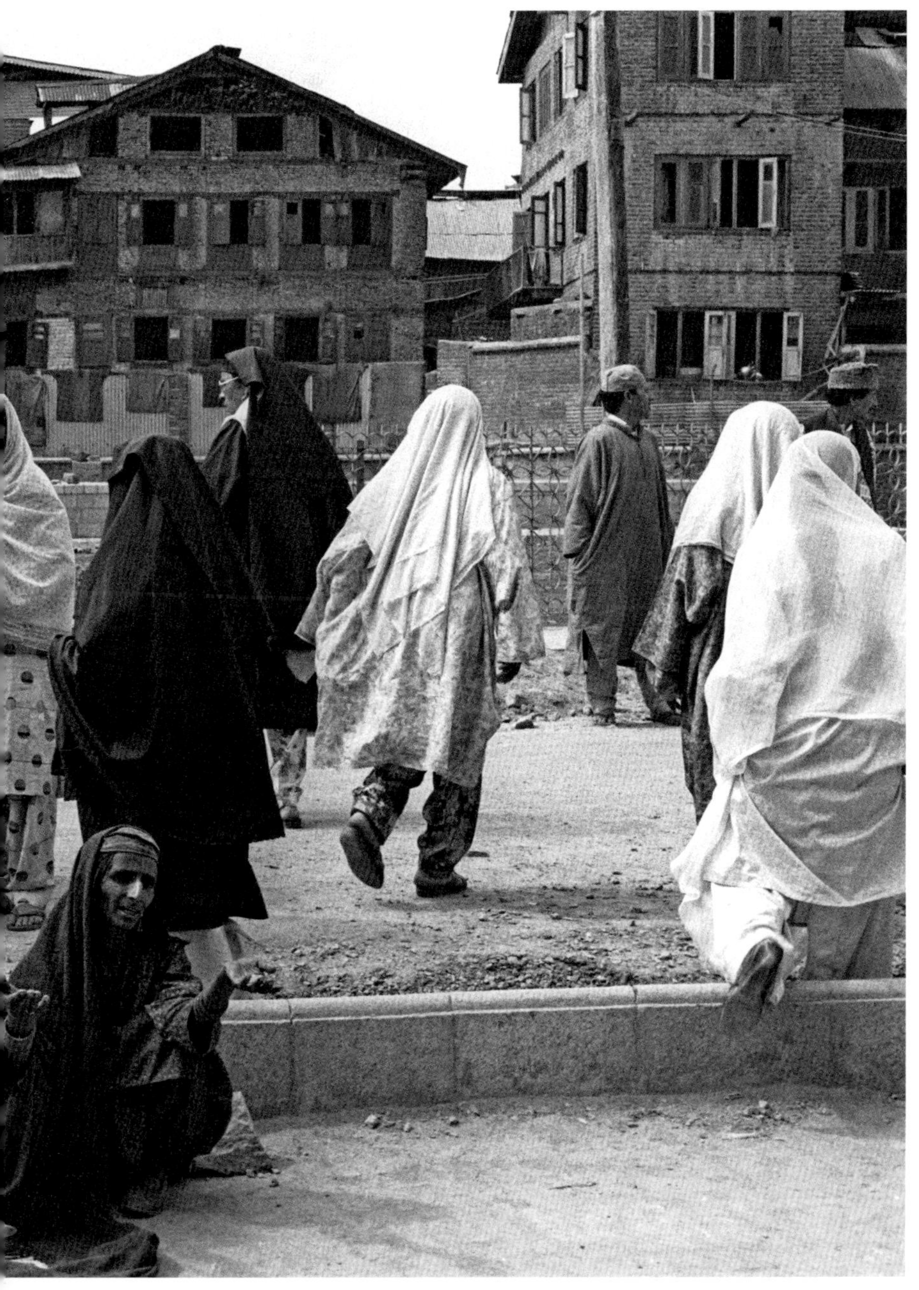

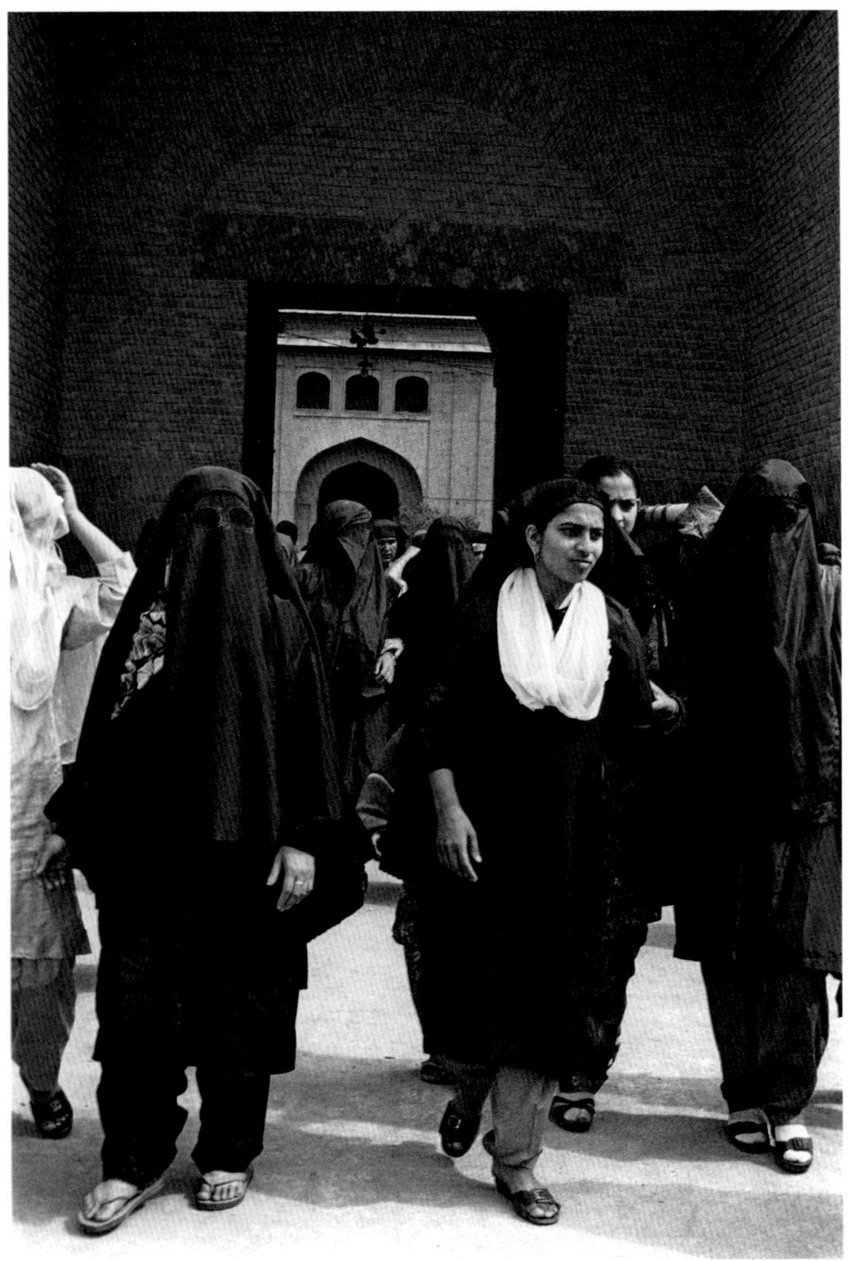

  Students leaving women's college, Srinagar, Kashmir

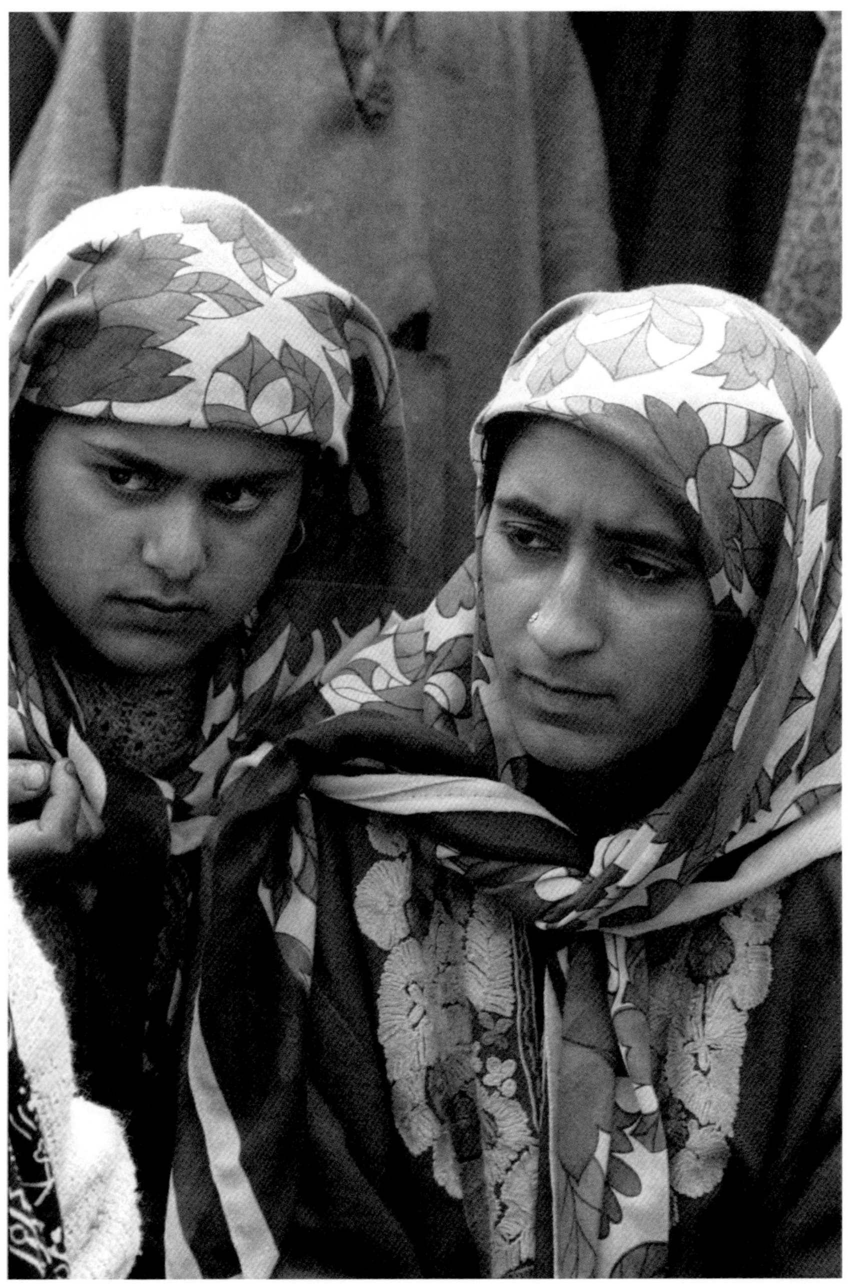

   Lala and Hammeda, Kupwara Village, Kashmir

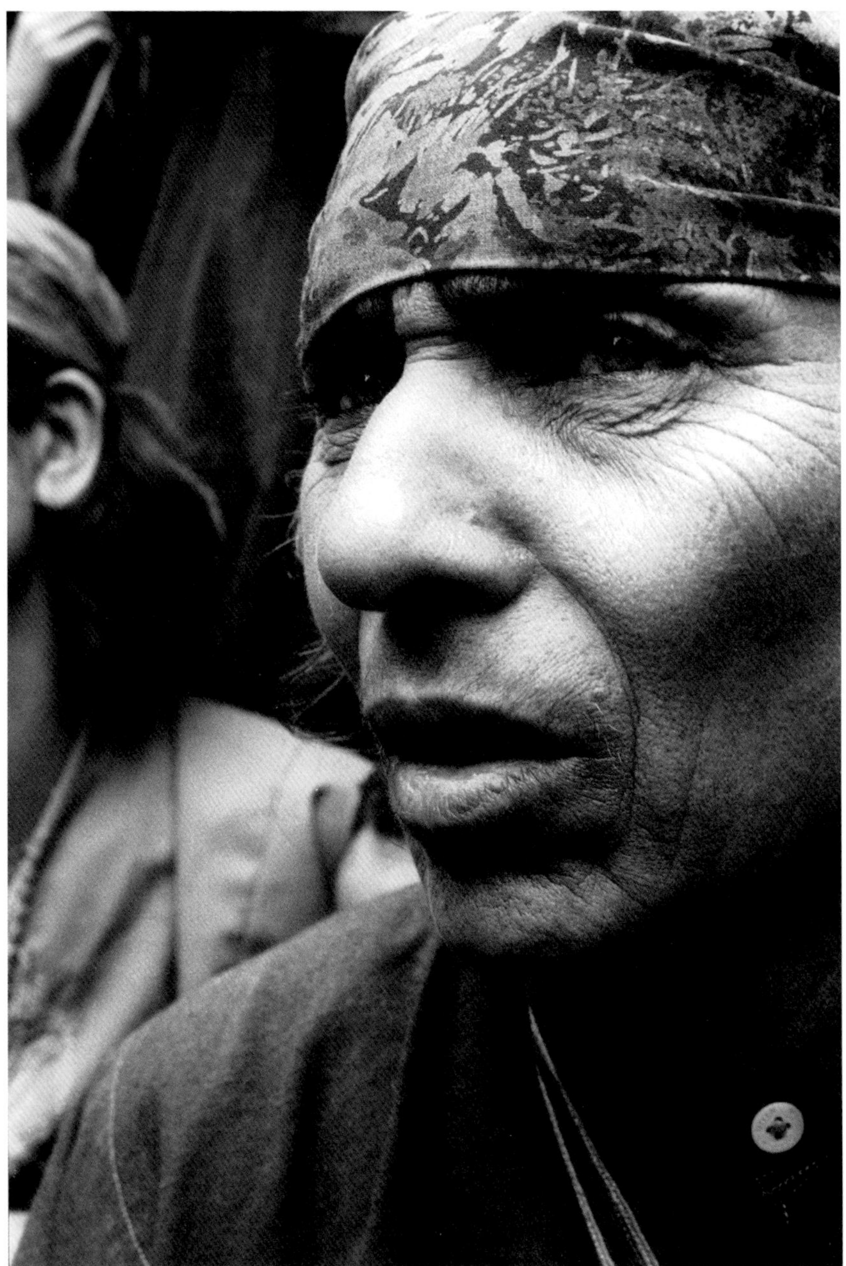

   Noor, Kupwara Village, Kashmir

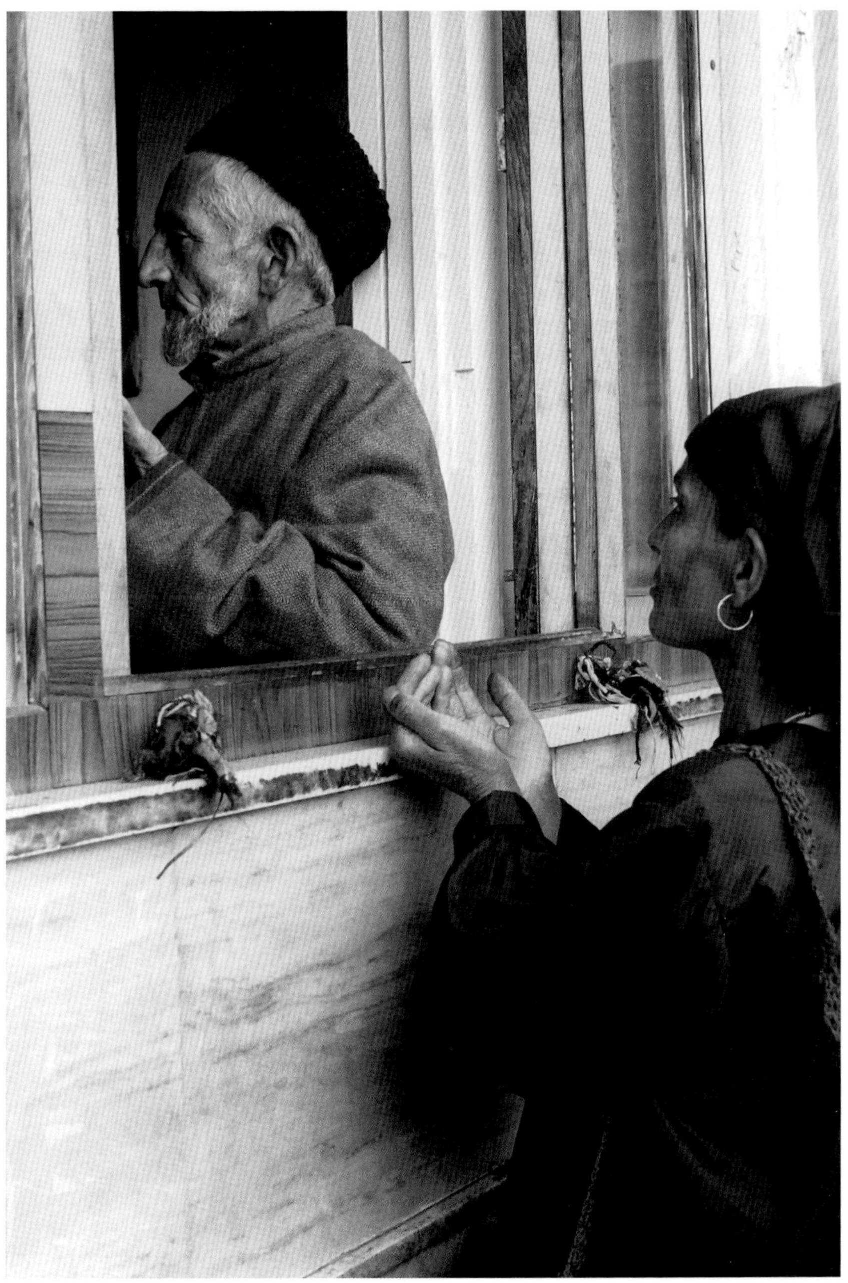

    Makhdoom Sahib, Sufi Shrine, Kashmir

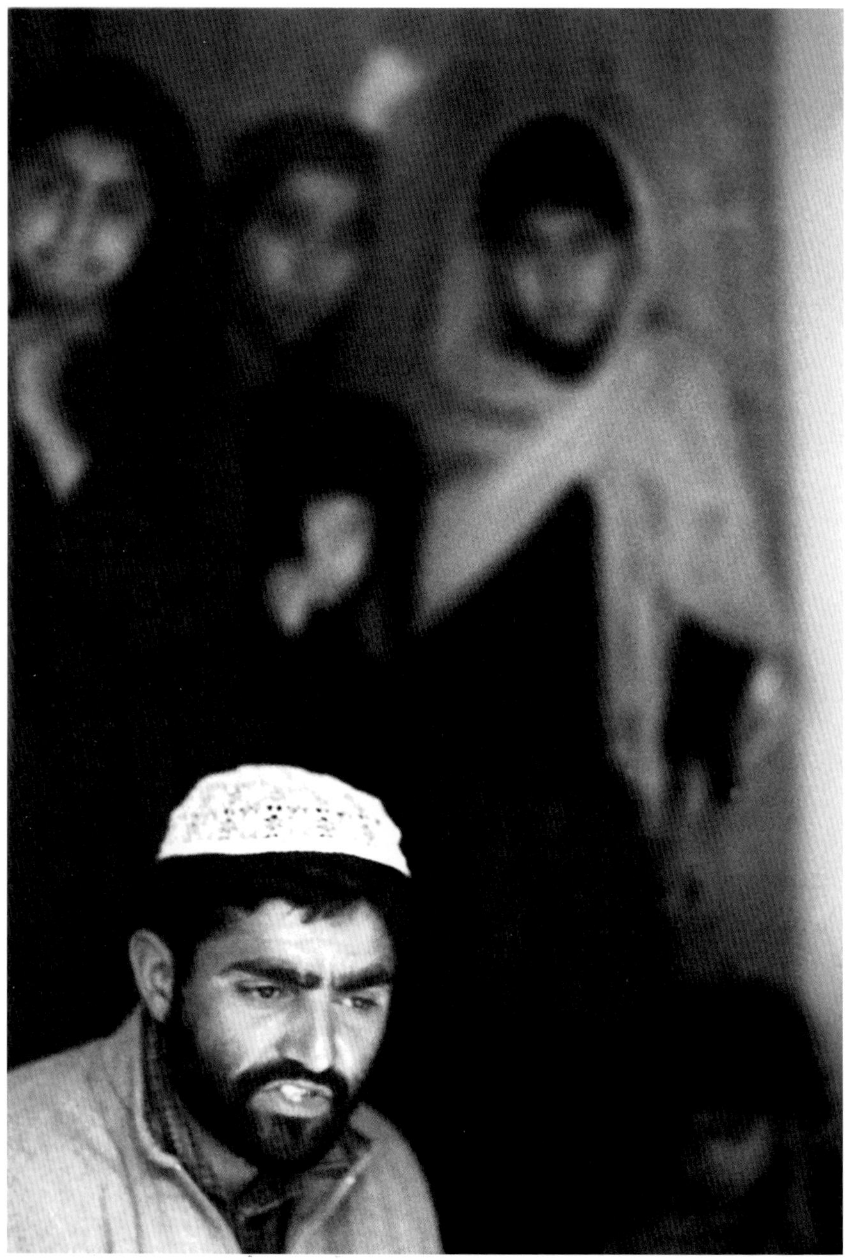

    Village Priest with women relatives, Malangam, Bandipora, Kashmir

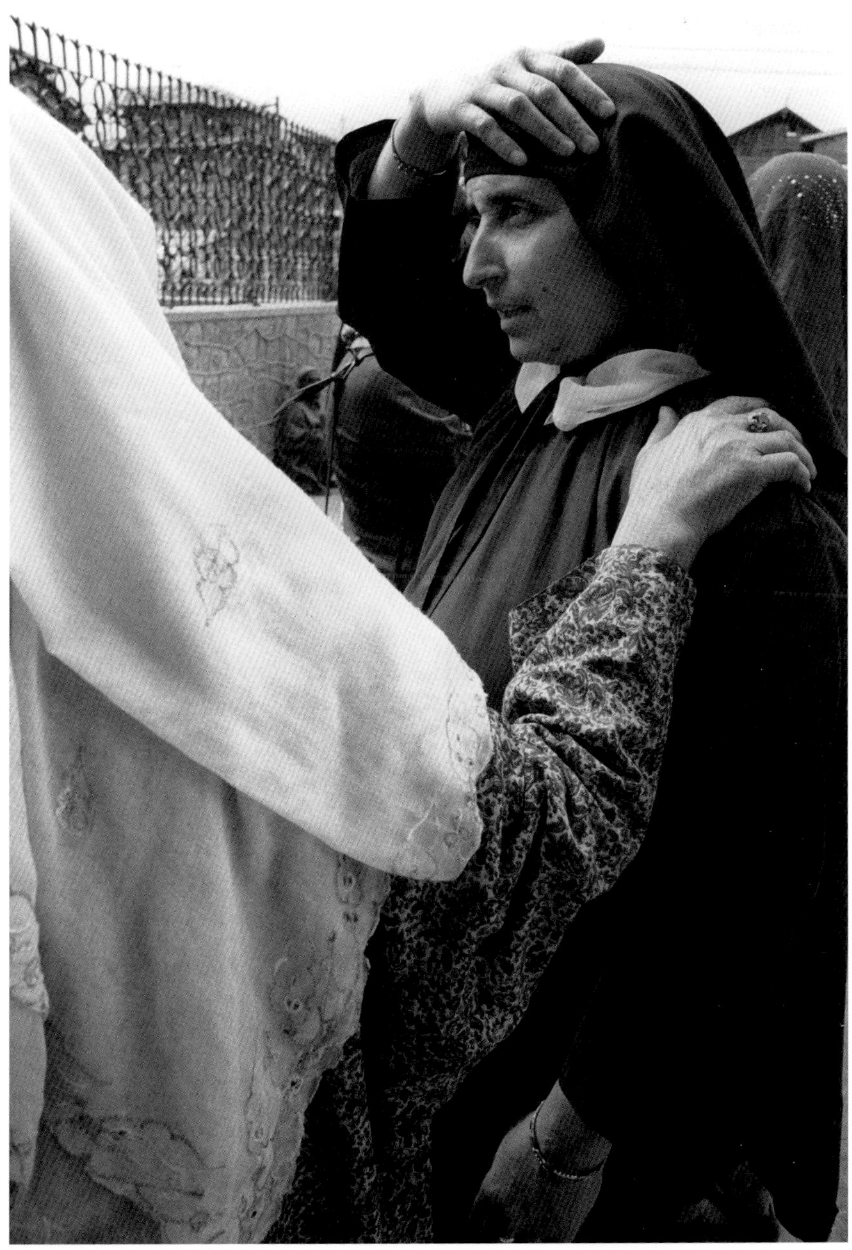

  Friends meeting after prayers, Jama Masjid, Srinagar, Kashmir

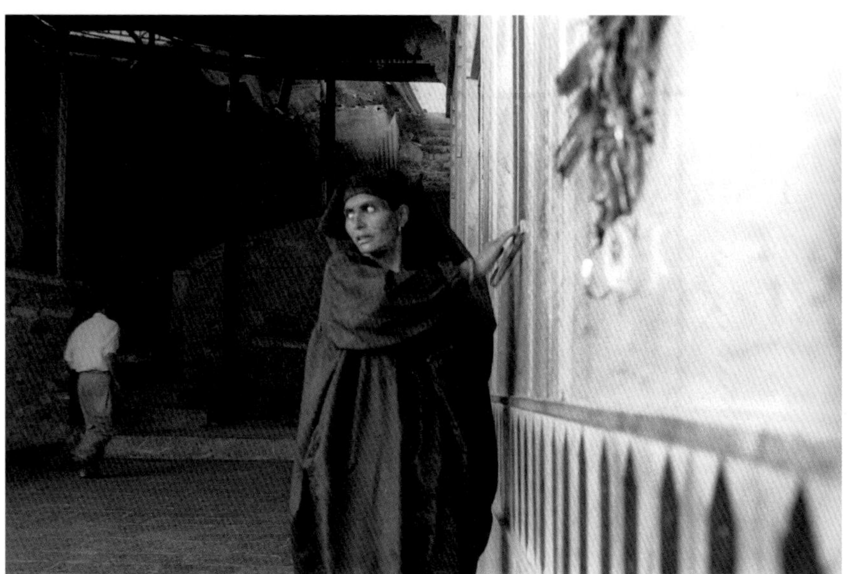

    Makhdoom Sahib, Sufi Shrine, Srinagar, Kashmir

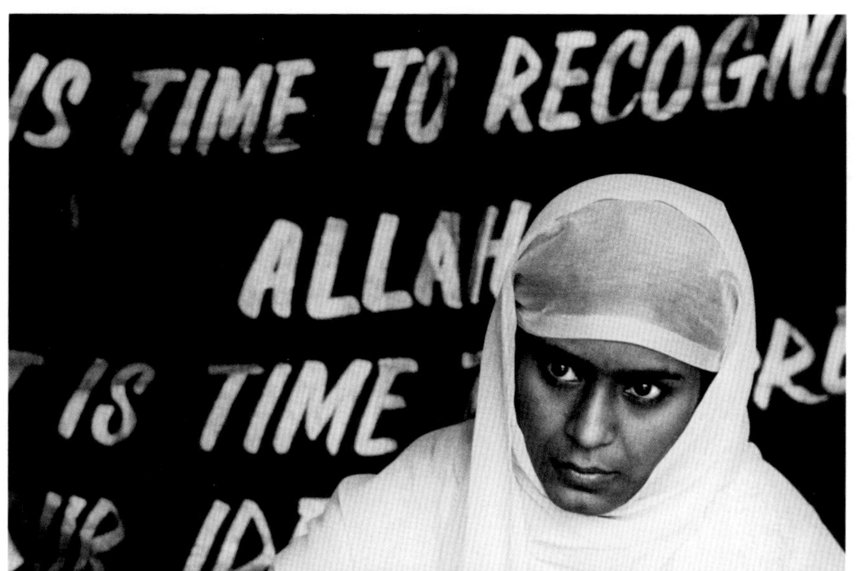

    Benazir, Khawateen Markaz, women's wing of the Hurriyat [political party], Srinagar, Kashmir

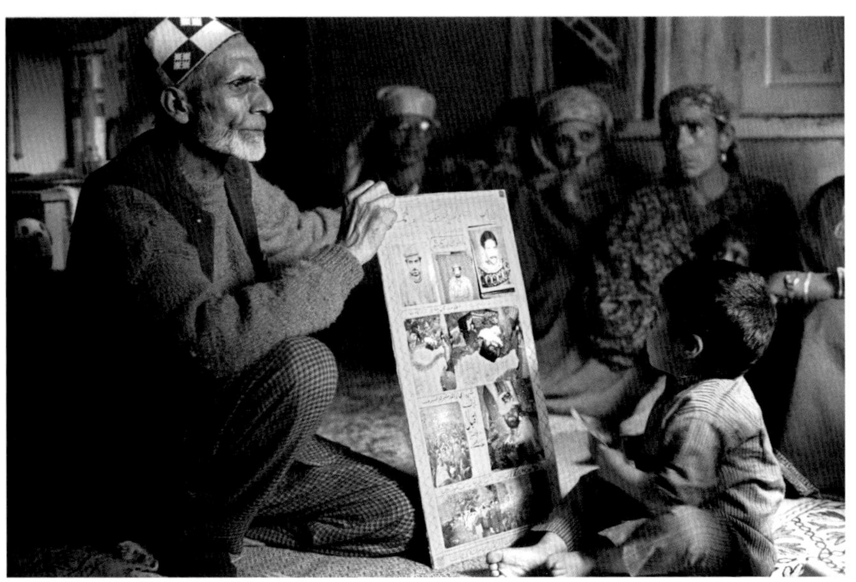

     Grandfather with collage glorifying son's death, Bandipora, Kashmir

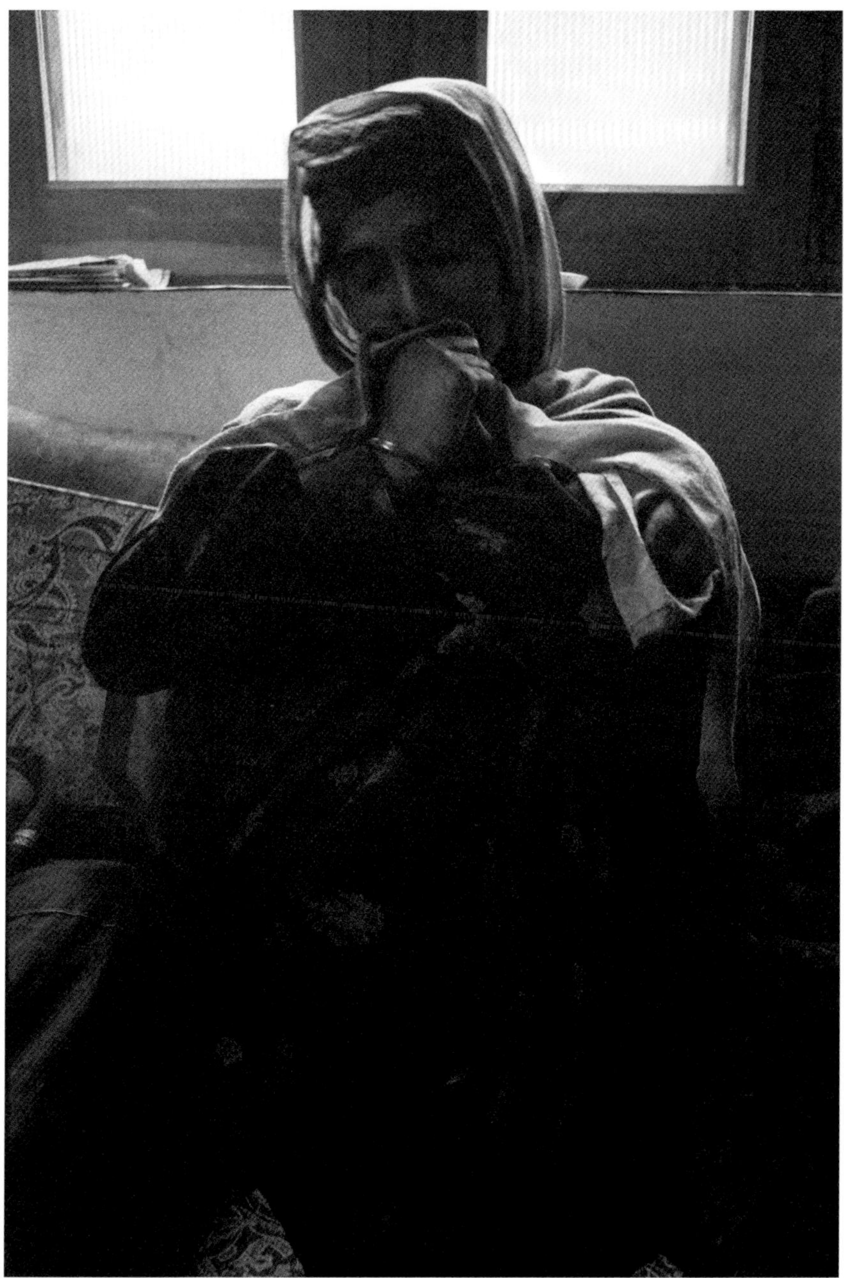

Hamida, half widow, Bandipora, Kashmir

INITIATION CHRONICLE

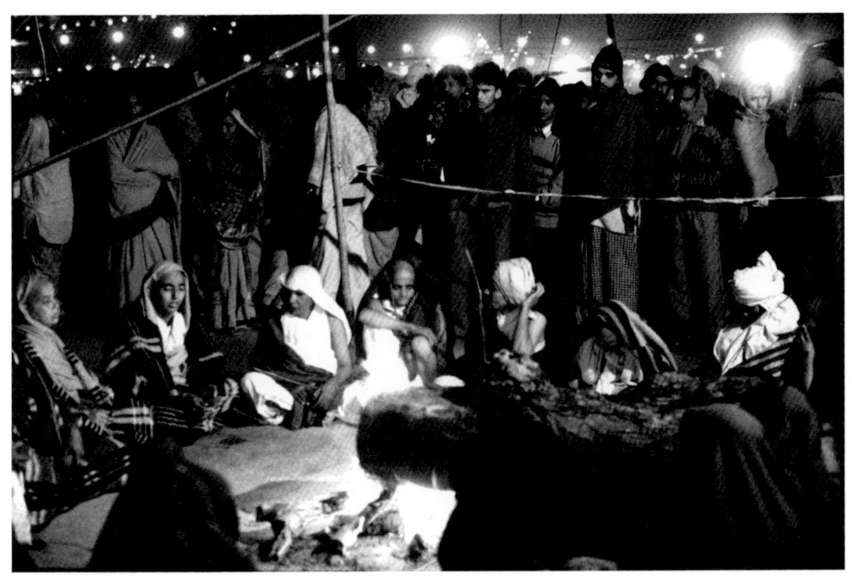

53

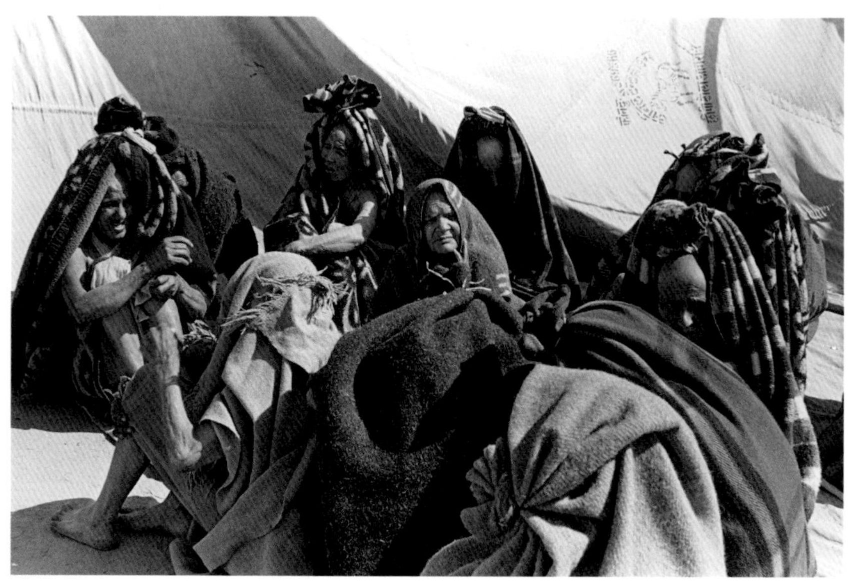

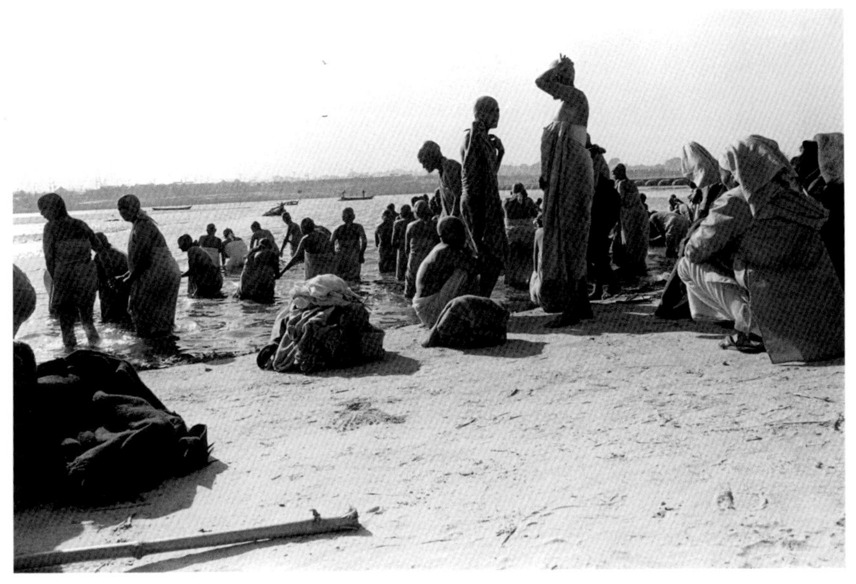

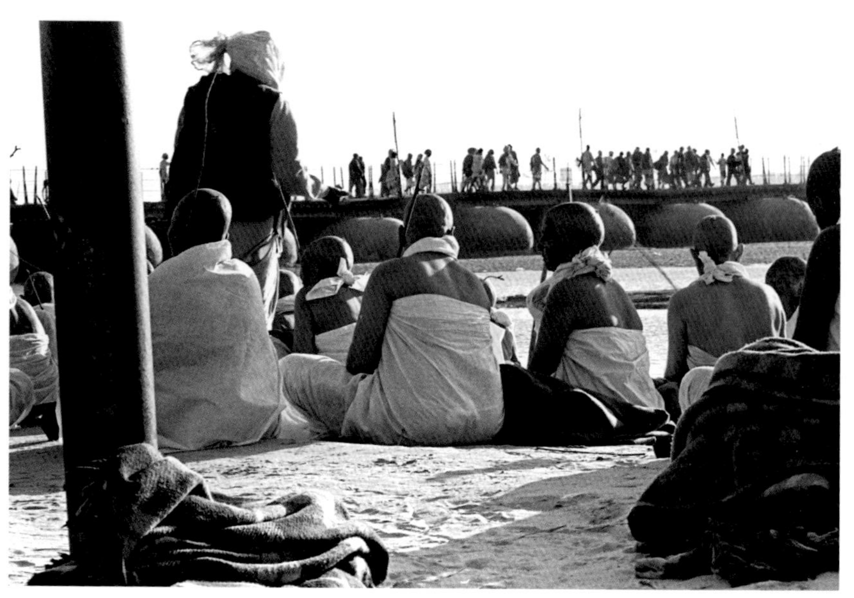

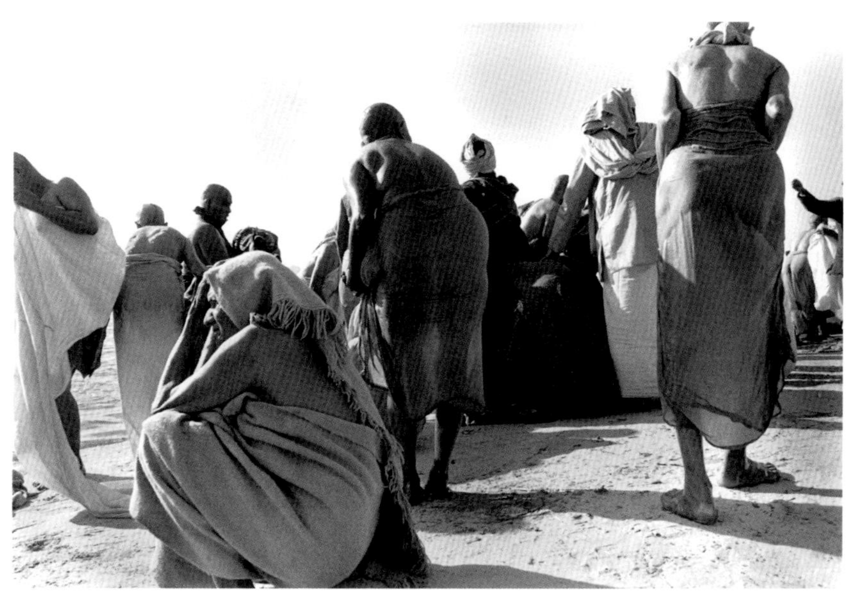

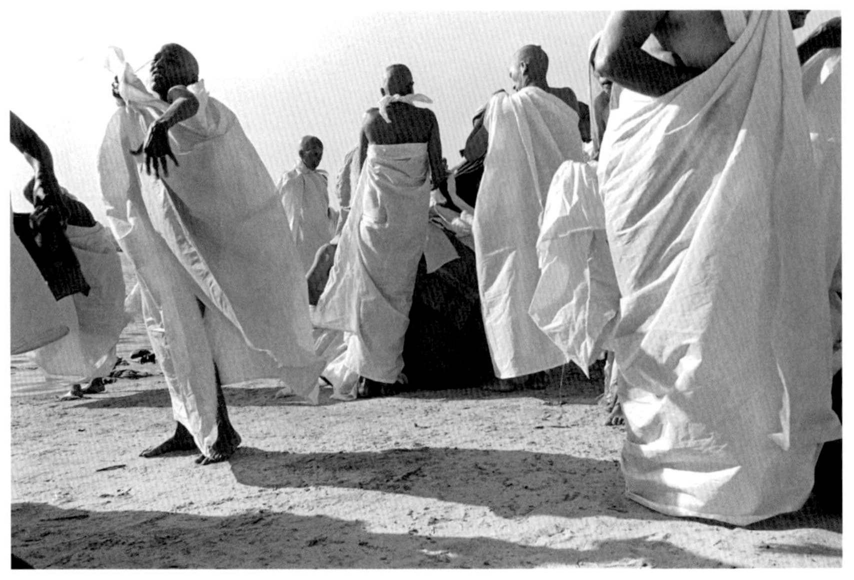

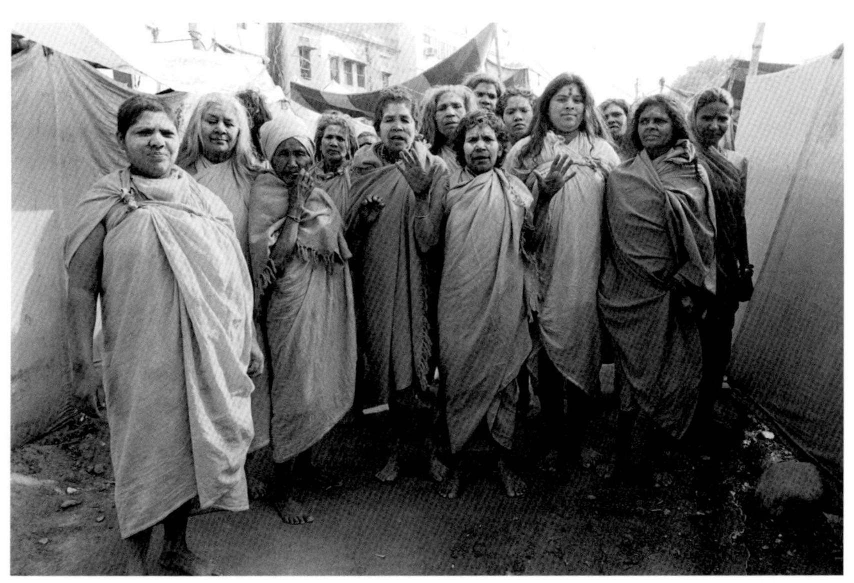

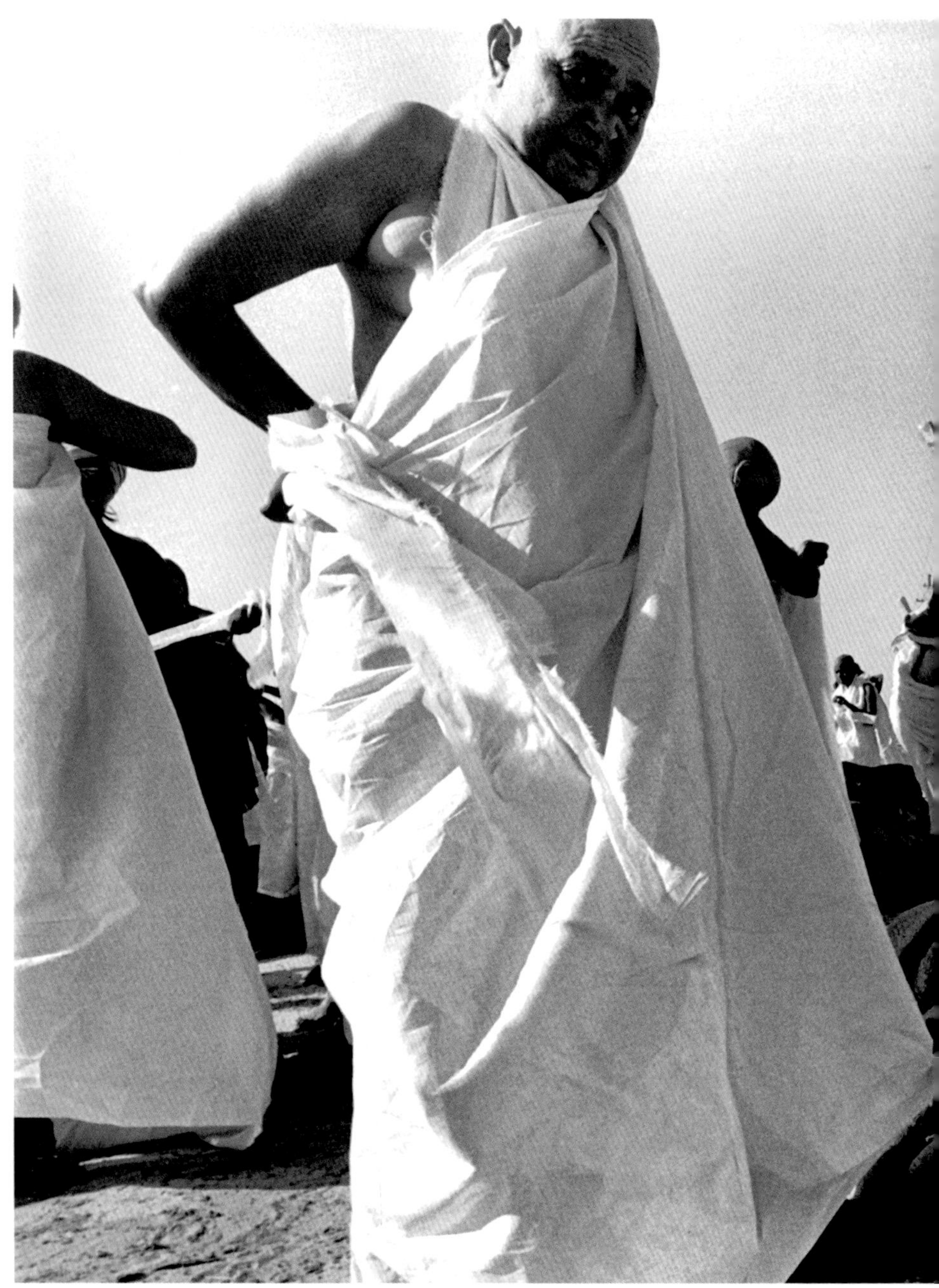

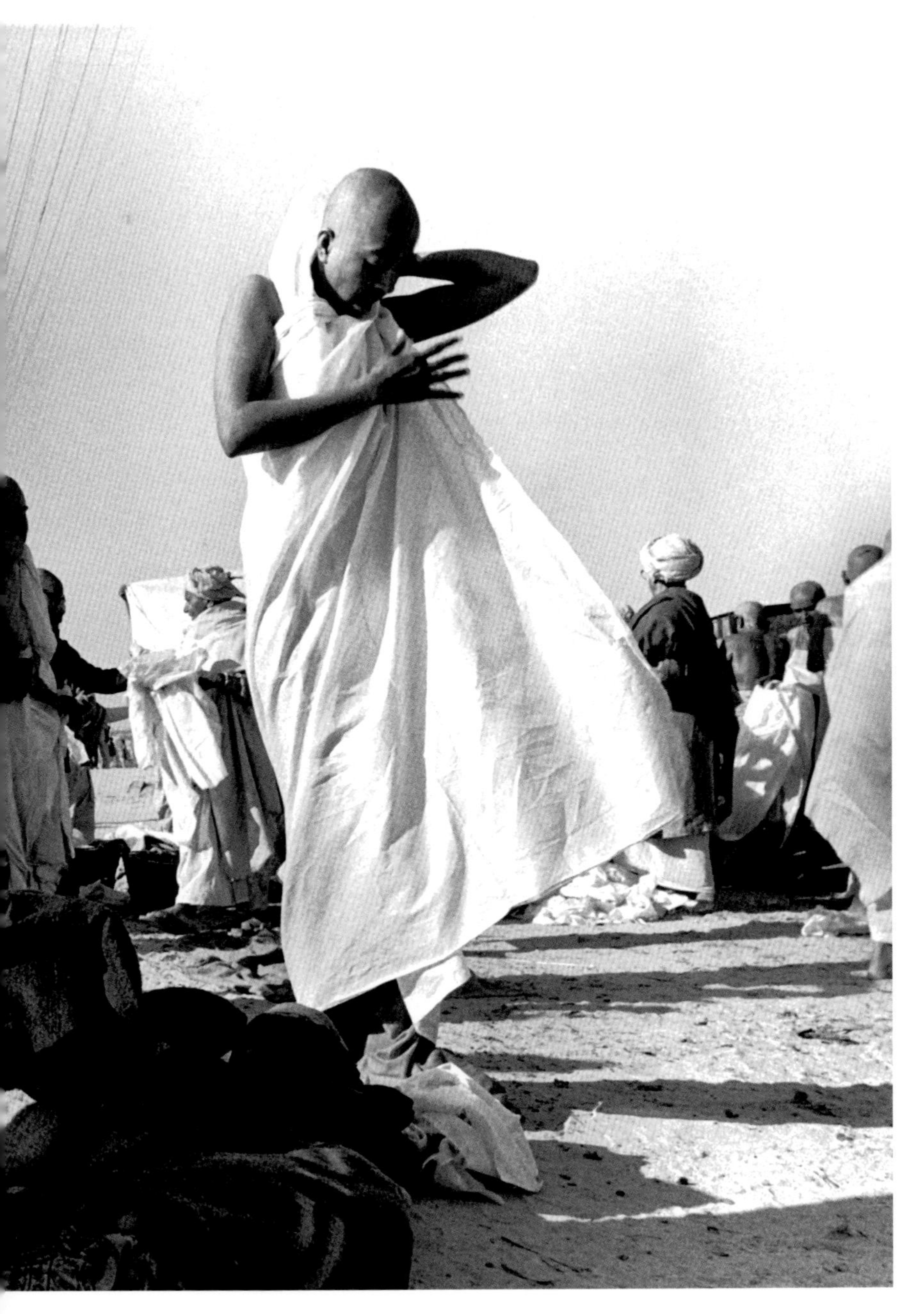

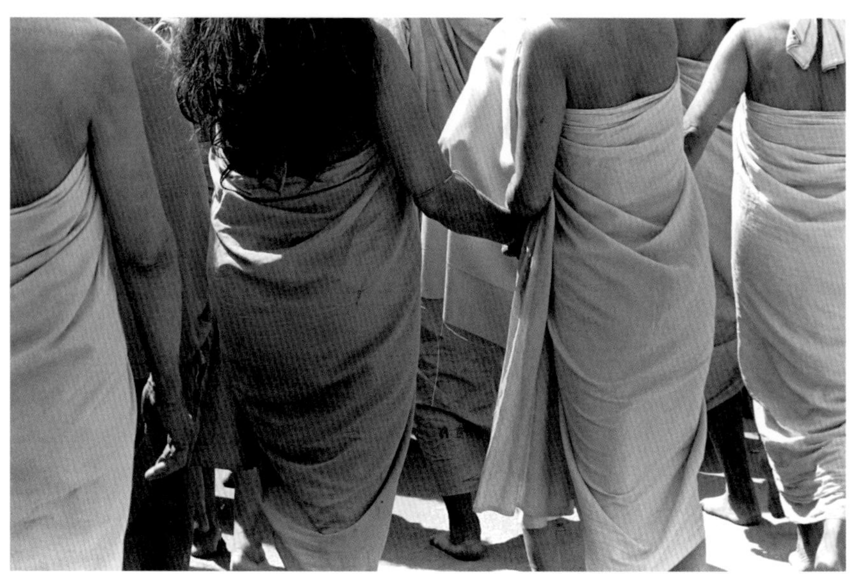

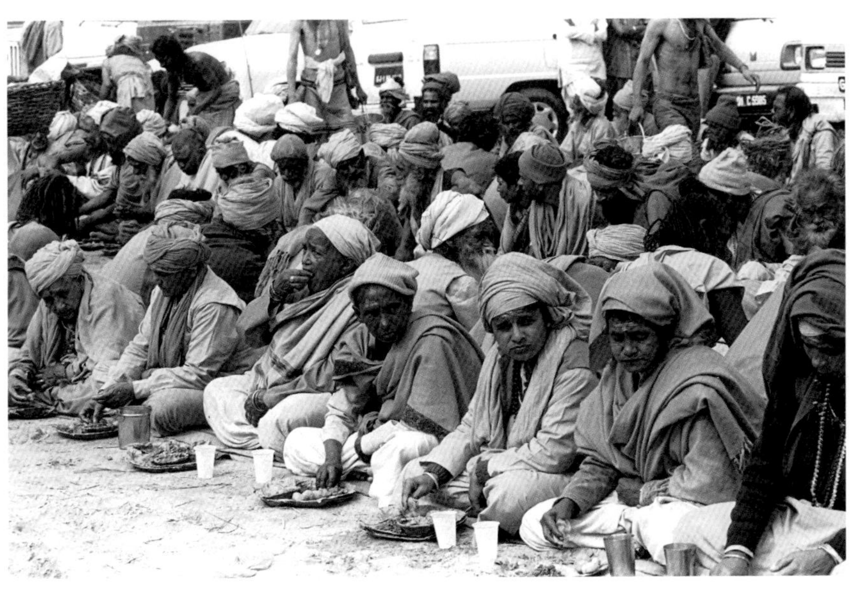

CREDITS

All artworks © Sheba Chhachhi 2022

Sequences of images reproduced in this book are selections from three series.

pp.17–33
Seven Lives and a Dream 1980–91
Photographs, gelatin silver print on paper
Overall display dimensions variable
Tate. Purchased using funds provided by the South Asia Acquisitions Committee and Tate Members 2014

pp.35–51
The Green of the Valley is Khaki 1994
Black and white photographs, archival pigment prints
Overall display dimensions variable
Private collection of the artist

pp.53–63
Initiation Chronicle 2001–7
Black and white photographs, archival pigment prints
Overall display dimensions variable
Private collection of the artist

ARTIST'S ACKNOWLEDGEMENTS

To all the women who have collaborated with me in making these photographs.